MODERN
Homesteading

LIVING THE
Country
Life

MODERN
Homesteading

Advice and inspiration for cultivating a better life.

Contents

Do-It-Yourself Recipes

Canning & Freezing

Small Livestock

Indoors: Live Naturally & Beautifully

Outdoor Projects

Introduction

Do you dream of having a farmhouse on a little piece of land in the country with a garden full of fresh vegetables, a raspberry bramble, and an endless supply of eggs from a flock of chickens? Are you already living that dream? Either way, this book is your guide to a better life. It's for those who desire to escape the chaos and overstimulation of city life and seek the peace of the country. It's for those who long to grow and raise their own food—and to prepare it in fresh, wholesome, unadulterated ways. It's for those who want to shepherd a flock of sheep or a herd of goats—and to learn the art of cheesemaking—or to plant a garden that will attract pollinators such as hummingbirds or bees. Get started as a beekeeper or a bunnykeeper. Make your own soap, herbal spa products, or a wine rack from reclaimed wood. The information, tips and projects in this user-friendly guide are relevant to anyone who seeks to cultivate a patch of paradise on earth—whether you have a rural zip code and are looking for practical advice or if you're an armchair homesteader who simply wants to bring a bit of the country into your life.

CHAPTER 1

Edible Gardening

Raising your own fruits and vegetables allows you to connect to the Earth in a personal way. And when you grow your own food, you'll be amazed at how fresh food can taste: Sun-warmed tomatoes, crisp apples, and savory greens have a flavor all their own when they are eaten moments after harvest. And you'll enjoy more choices: You can grow exotic heirlooms and new varieties that you can't find in grocery stores.

1

PLANT FLOWERS WITH FOOD

Interplant flowers with vegetables to create a beautiful (and delicious!) garden. Experiment with planting in blocks and clusters rather than rows for a more decorative effect.

2
KNOW YOUR SOIL

Identify your soil type and then determine the best way to improve it.

How would you characterize your soil? Is it poor, boggy muck that drains poorly and lacks nutrients? Could it be the red clay of Georgia, the sandy clay of Texas, or the caliche (sandy, rocky, alkaline stuff) of Arizona? You must identify your soil before improving it–whether it needs fertility, absorbency, or drainability. Here are soil options:

LOAM The ideal soil holds air, water, and nutrients in a balance of sand, silt, clay, and organic matter. It's easy to work. A handful of loam holds its shape when squeezed and crumbles when squeezed harder. If well-drained, it leaches nutrients and warms slowly. Add worm castings, rotted manure, and organic matter (compost and chopped leaves) to improve it.

CLAY This heavy, poorly draining stuff forms a sticky, hard mass when squeezed. Plant roots have a hard time growing in clay soil; they may die due to lack of air and water. Improve it with loads of organic matter, such as grass clippings, chopped leaves, old hay, ground bark or wood shavings, and gypsum.

SAND Sand holds too much air; it holds neither water nor nutrients. A handful crumbles and won't form a ball. It tills easily and warms up quickly. Improve it by adding organic matter: compost, rotted manure, and chopped leaves.

3
TEST, TESTING 1-2-3

Soil testing sounds difficult and fussy and technical, but it's actually pretty simple. Here's how to do it:

STEP 1 Fill a quart (1 L) jar about one-third full with soil. Then fill the rest of the jar with water. Screw on the lid.

STEP 2 Give the jar a robust shake to break up the clumps.

STEP 3 Put the jar down. Do nothing–unless you want to watch it settle. Let it sit overnight.

STEP 4 Grab a permanent marker. Draw on the jar where the level of the sand is. Then draw a line where there's silt and, finally, clay.

Those lines can help you approximate what your soil is. Loam should be about 30 to 40 percent sand, 30 to 40 percent loam, and 20 percent clay.

4

BUILD BETTER SOIL

Apply amendments individually or in combination each season. Spread compost, manure, and peat 3 inches (8 cm) deep on top of soil and work into the top 3 to 6 inches (8 to 15 cm); apply ½ inch (12 mm) or less of sand, greensand, and vermiculite, perlite, or gypsum; and work into the top 8 inches (20 cm) of soil.

These materials help improve soil's fertility and its capacity to hold and drain moisture:

COMPOST Decomposed leaves, grass clippings, plant-based kitchen scraps, and other organic materials. A well-balanced, slow-release, nutrient- and humus-rich amendment. Lightens heavy soils; enriches poor soil.

SAND Coarse sand in small amounts improves drainage and loosens clay soil. Too much sand turns some soils into concrete. Contains no nutrients but lasts indefinitely.

MANURE Aged or rotted manure (from cows, horses, sheep, goats, chicken, or pigs) boosts levels of soil nitrogen, loosens heavy soil, and improves water retention in light soils. Fresh manure burns plants; compost it for a full year before using.

PEAT Absorbs moisture; especially helpful in sandy soil. Loosens heavy or clay soils. If allowed to dry out, it can become hard, crusty, and difficult to remoisten, so keep it lightly damp. Peat or peat moss may be harvested from environmentally fragile peat bogs, a limited resource. Use sphagnum peat moss instead.

VERMICULITE Made by heating mica until it bursts, this lightweight particulate holds moisture and loosens soil. Good in all soil types. Lasts indefinitely.

PERLITE White volcanic residue that aerates soil and lasts indefinitely. Good for all soil types; a little helps.

GREENSAND Powdered rock that contains potassium and other nutrients. Slows soil compaction and helps retain moisture.

GYPSUM Powdered mineral that loosens heavy and clay soil; improves drainage. Gypsum is useful in changing the texture of soil that has been packed down by heavy traffic, flooding, or weather.

GET A NUTRIENT BOOST

Basic Nutrients Fertilizers contain all of the basic nutrients: nitrogen, phosphorus, and potassium. These are listed on packaged plant foods in percentages of N-P-K. Or add these organic materials to soil.

Nitrogen (N) Sources for Leaf and Stem Growth Alfalfa meal, blood meal, composted manure, cottonseed meal, feather meal, fish meal or emulsion, mushroom compost, rice hulls

Phosphorus (P) Sources for Root Growth, Flower Color, and Disease Resistance Bat guano, bonemeal, rock phosphate

Potassium (K) Sources for Fruit and Seed Production Dolomite lime, greens and, kelp meal, oyster-shell lime, rock dust, seaweed, wood ashes

BE IN THE KNOW: WHAT'S YOUR SOIL pH?

GET TESTING Buy a soil pH test kit from a garden center. Follow the instructions in the kit. The pH scale describes the degree of acidity or alkalinity of the soil. An extremely high (alkaline) or low (acid) pH affects the ability of a plant to absorb essential mineral nutrients from the soil.

RAISE pH To raise the pH of acid soil, add ground limestone from a local garden center or hardware store (this process is called "sweetening the soil").

LOWER pH To lower the pH of alkaline soil, use powdered sulfur, acid peat moss, or an acid fertilizer.

6

CREATE COMPOST

It's easy to cook up your own compost. Layer organic materials–garden clippings, dry leaves, kitchen vegetable scraps, shredded paper–and a dash of soil to create a concoction that turns into humus, the best soil builder around.

Before you start piling on, recognize that there are two types of composting: cold and hot. Cold composting is as simple as collecting yard waste or taking out the organic materials in your trash (such as fruit and vegetable peels, coffee grounds and filters, and eggshells) and then corralling them in a pile or bin. Over the course of a year or so, the material will decompose.

Hot composting is for the more serious gardener, and you get compost in one to three months during warm weather. Four ingredients are required for fast-cooking hot compost: nitrogen, carbon, air, and water. Together, these items feed microorganisms, which speed up the process of decay.

Good household materials to compost include fruit and vegetable scraps, eggshells, coffee grounds, shredded newspaper, and sawdust from untreated wood.

Good outdoor materials include dry leaves, finely chopped wood and bark chips, straw, and grass and plant clippings.

HOW TO CREATE AND USE HOT COMPOST

STEP 1 To create your own organic hot-compost heap, wait until you have enough materials to make a pile at least 3 feet (1 m) deep. Then, to ensure an even composition of materials, create alternating 4- to 8-inch-deep (10–20 cm) layers of green materials (kitchen scraps, fresh leaves, coffee grounds) and brown materials (dried leaves, shredded paper, untreated sawdust).

STEP 2 Sprinkle water over the pile regularly so it has the consistency of a damp sponge. Don't add too much water or the microorganisms will become waterlogged and drown. Your pile will rot instead of compost.

Check to see if your pile is decomposing by monitoring temperature. Check the temperature of the pile with a thermometer or simply reach into the middle of the pile with your hand.

STEP 3 During the growing season, provide the pile with oxygen by turning it once a week with a garden fork. The best time to turn compost is when the center of the pile feels warm or the thermometer reads between 130°F and 150°F

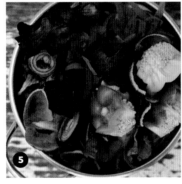

(54°–66°C). Stirring the pile helps it cook faster and prevents material from becoming matted down and developing a bad odor. At this point, the layers have created equal amounts of green and brown materials throughout the pile, so stir thoroughly.

STEP 4 When the compost no longer gives off heat and becomes dry, brown, and crumbly, it's ready.

DON'T COMPOST

- Anything containing meat, oil, fat, or grease
- Diseased plant materials
- Sawdust or chips from pressure-treated wood
- Dog or cat feces
- Weeds that go to seed
- Dairy products

PLAN YOUR VEGETABLE GARDEN

Starting a vegetable garden at home gives you the pleasure of savoring a delicious, sun-warmed tomato fresh from the garden. In almost every case, the flavor and texture of varieties you can grow far exceed grocery store produce.

If you plan it right, you can enjoy a beautiful garden full of the fruits of your labor–without having to spend hours and hours tending it.

DECIDE WHAT TO PLANT

When deciding what to plant in a garden with vegetables, it's best to start small, so you can figure out what works best for you.

So first, take a look at how much your family will eat when you think about how to plan a vegetable garden. Keep in mind that vegetables such as tomatoes, peppers, and squash keep providing throughout the season, so you may not need many plants to serve your needs.

Other vegetables, such as carrots, radishes, and corn, produce only once and, as a result, you may need to plant more of these.

DETERMINE HOW MUCH SPACE YOU NEED

Once you know what you want to plant, you can figure out how to plan a vegetable garden with the right amount of space.

Keep in mind when determining what to plant that you don't need a large space to begin. If you choose to grow in containers, you don't even need a yard–a deck or balcony may provide plenty of space.

In fact, a well-tended 10×10-foot (3×3-m) vegetable garden will usually produce more than a weed-filled or disease-ridden 25×50-foot (8×15-m) bed.

PICK THE PERFECT SPOT

There are three basic requirements for success no matter how big your vegetable garden is or what you plant in it:

FULL SUN Most vegetables need at least 6 to 8 hours of direct sun. If they don't get enough light, they won't bear as much and they'll be more susceptible to attack from insects or diseases.

If you don't have a spot in full sun to plant a garden with vegetables, you can still grow many leafy vegetables such as lettuce and spinach. And if you're in a hot-summer climate, cool-season varieties such as peas may do better in part shade.

PLENTY OF WATER Because most vegetables aren't very drought-tolerant, you'll need to give them a drink during dry spells. When thinking about how to plan a vegetable garden, remember: The closer your garden is to a source of water, the easier it will be for you.

GOOD SOIL As with any kind of garden, success usually starts with the soil. Most vegetables do best in moist, well-drained soil that's rich in organic matter (such as compost or peat moss).

Many gardeners like to have their vegetable gardens close to the house. This makes it easier to harvest fresh produce while you're cooking.

GO ORGANIC

Enjoy healthy, tasty, organic vegetables fresh from your garden. Try these tips for success.

FEED YOUR PLANTS NATURALLY In most soils, fertilizing your vegetables isn't necessary, but it will help them grow faster and give you better crops. If you feed your plants, choose natural products. Well-rotted animal manure from plant-eating critters (rabbits, horses, sheep, pigs, cows, chickens) is a great source. Or look for prepackaged organic materials online or at your local garden center.

Note: If you have rich soil already, it may be best not to fertilize. Too much of a good thing can make your plants put on lots of lush, soft growth that's loved by pests. Slower-growing plants often resist insects and disease better.

PRACTICE ROTATION If you plant the same vegetables in the same spot every year, disease can build up and be ready before your plants have much of a chance. Keep the element of surprise against your disease foes and try to plant your crops in different parts of the garden each year.

Because many closely related plants are affected by the same diseases, avoid planting them where their relatives were the year or two before. Two of the biggest families are the tomato family (tomatoes, peppers, potatoes, eggplant) and the squash family (squash, pumpkin, cucumber, watermelon).

MULCH WELL A layer of mulch not only helps reduce weeds, but it also creates a barrier that can prevent fungal disease spores from splashing up onto plant leaves. In most cases, a layer of mulch 1 to 2 inches (2.5–5 cm) thick is best.

BEST PLANTS FOR ATTRACTING BENEFICIAL INSECTS

1. Bachelor's button
2. Cleome
3. Cosmos
4. Black-eyed Susan
5. Daisy
6. Marigold
7. Nasturtium
8. Purple coneflower
9. Salvia
10. Sunflower
11. Yarrow
12. Zinnia

For an extra bonus, use a mulch made from an organic material that will slowly decompose through the growing season (such as cocoa hulls or weed-free straw). As it breaks down, it adds organic matter to the soil for you–meaning you may have one less garden task to do.

9

START YOUR OWN SEEDS

Planting seeds indoors has practical benefits: saving money, getting a head start on the growing season, and selecting from varieties more diverse than those available at your local garden center. There are also the seemingly magical benefits of the joy and wonder that come with watching an innocuous seed sprout into a living plant. You will be so amazed and proud!

Knowing that your garden plants can be grown from seeds or seedlings (transplants), think ahead. When the outdoor world remains wintry, start vegetables, herbs, and flowers from seeds indoors. Then be alert in spring to favorable conditions to sow them directly in the garden.

When purchasing seeds, check packets for freshness dates and choose the best varieties for your garden and climate. It's easy to get carried away and purchase too many seed packets. What's more, a packet of seeds includes dozens—even hundreds—of potential plants and most likely more than you will need for this year's garden. Buy only what you need and have room to raise, then save leftover seeds for next year or share them with friends and neighbors.

Seed packets contain all the planting details needed: seed spacing, depth, number of days until maturity, and much more. Plant seeds in damp soilless seed-starting medium, following directions on the seed packet for the appropriate planting depth. Seedlings root quickly and stay healthier when grown in a sterile, fine-textured seed-starting mix rather than soil. Commercial seed-starting mix, available from garden suppliers and nurseries, usually includes peat moss, perlite, and vermiculite. Pop-up containers (above) made from peat moss pellets provide another option. Premoisten the medium—whether bulk seed-starting mix or pellets—by sprinkling it with warm water, then fill containers with damp mix.

GET A JUMP-START INDOORS

Sow seeds for heat-loving, slow-growing vegetables indoors about 8 weeks before the soil is warm enough to plant them outside.

EGGPLANT

Eggplant comes in a surprising number of varieties. And they're not all purple.

JAPANESE WHITE EGG This Asian variety bears 2- to 3-inch (5–8 cm) white oval fruits, which is a good size for stir-frying.

ROSA BIANCAIS This Italian heirloom is prized for its lavender color and mild flavor.

TOMATO

Heirloom varieties and unusual new hybrids offer almost every color of the rainbow and a delicious array of flavors.

FANTASTICO offers high yields of sweet red cherry tomatoes.

RED ZEBRA is a gorgeous heirloom with red skin and orange stripes. The 3-inch (8 cm) fruits have outstanding flavor.

PEPPER

Branch out from the usual bell pepper with a wider range of sweetness and heat.

MAMA MIA GIALLO This variety offers stunning yields of 7- to 9-inch-long (18–23 cm) fruits that are golden when ripe.

SWEET SUNSET A new banana type that bears loads of crisp, mild fruits that ripen to red.

SOW DIRECTLY

Certain seeds sprout and grow so quickly that you gain little by starting them indoors. Root crops such as carrots and beets don't like to be transplanted because their taproots are fragile when young. Sow these directly in the ground.

CUCUMBER

Let vigorous vines ramble over the ground or climb up a trellis to save space. Bush types can be grown in containers.

LEMON This heirloom bears pale yellow fruits the size of lemons.

BUSH SLICER This compact variety likes growing in a pot. The 6- to 8-inch (15–20 cm) fruits are sweet and crisp.

SWEET CORN

Sweet corn is plentiful and inexpensive in high season, so use your space for rarer varieties both edible and ornamental.

STRAWBERRY CORN This popular for fall decor and delicious when popped.

FIELD OF DREAMS This has attractive striped foliage and small but flavorful popped kernels.

SUGAR PEARL This sweet, early-maturing corn has all-white kernels.

LETTUCE

Though lettuce can be started indoors, most sow this cool-season crop directly in the ground as soon as soil is workable.

LITTLE GEM Each head of this cold- and heat-tolerant mini romaine is a single serving.

LOLLO ROSSO This cut-and-come-again looseleaf type has ruffled burgundy leaves.

FOUR SEASONS Also called Merveille des Quatre Saisons, this is a French heirloom Bibb.

10

PLANT INTENSIVELY

The surest way to increase the yield from a vegetable garden is to reduce the space between plants. The idea is to plant wide bands, thus reducing the amount of ground devoted to paths.

To start an intensive garden, make a bed of any length, but limit its width to 3 to 4 feet (1–1.25 m)across so you can reach the center of the bed from either side. Although it's not necessary to box in the bed, it's a good idea. When you enclose a bed with vertical boards, it's not only neater, but the soil won't collapse onto the paths. It will also be easier for you to install row covers or erect supports for vertical growing.

WHAT YOU NEED

String, small sticks or dowels, trowel or dibble, seedlings, water

STEP 1 Before planting the bed, prepare the soil by digging at

least 8 to 12 inches (20–30 cm) and turning over shovelfuls to loosen and aerate it. Add in organic matter, such as compost or manure–the more organic matter you mix in, the better.

Then run lines of string to establish a grid. The grid will help you position young plants at the proper distance from one another.

STEP 2 Use a trowel or dibble to dig holes for transplant-size vegetables. Gently remove the seedling from its container, then grasp the leaves to guide it while supporting the root ball.

Set the plant in the hole at

the same depth at which it was growing in its container. Firm the soil gently over the roots around the stem. This will help put the roots in contact with the soil.

Make evenly spaced depressions in the soil with your finger if you are planting seeds. Be sure to follow the recommendations on the seed packet to know how deep to make the depressions.

STEP 3 Water well. For transplants, apply a gentle shower using a watering can or hose-end sprayer. For seeds, use the lightest setting on a hose-end sprayer to avoid disturbing the soil.

11

INTERPLANT FOR LARGER YIELDS

This technique takes advantage of the fact that some vegetables grow quickly and others take their time. For example, if you plant carrots and radishes together, you can harvest the radishes in about 30 days, when the carrots will still be quite small. You can also

combine a vertical vegetable (like tomatoes) with a low-growing crop (melons, for example).

SMART COMBINATIONS

- Grow sprawling melons and squash under stake-grown tomatoes.
- Surround corn with lettuce or peas with radishes.
- Combine quick and slow vegetables such as lettuce with tomatoes, and beets with pole beans, and spinach with winter squash.

12

GROW UP!

You'll find that some vegetables grow better with support. They do well on trellises, fences, and other structures. By growing up instead of out over the ground, your garden will produce more per square foot (.09 sq m). Vegetable plants grown up on a support also tend to suffer fewer disease problems.

Here are some of the most popular vegetables suited to vertical gardening.

TOMATOES Choose indeterminate varieties, which continue to grow and produce over a long period–often until frost.

Grow tomatoes in wire cages or support them by tying them to 7-foot-tall (2-m) wood stakes driven 2 feet (60 cm) into the ground. Cage-grown tomatoes require minimal attention but are more prone to fungal diseases. Tomatoes grown on stakes benefit from being pruned to a single stem; this means constantly pinching out new branches that arise in the crotch between the main stem and a leaf.

POLE BEANS Although they take longer to mature than bush-type beans, pole beans produce over a longer period. Train beans up tall wooden poles or a bamboo tipi.

CUCUMBERS Vine-type cucumbers (as opposed to the bush varieties) do well on fences and trellises.

Vertically grown cucumber fruits also tend to be straighter and more uniform in size and shape than those grown on the ground.

SNAP PEAS These supersweet edible pod peas are among the most productive vegetables in the spring garden. By selecting tall vining varieties (such as the original Sugar Snap pea), you can easily grow them on a 5- to 6-foot- (1.5–1.8m) tall mesh trellis. Pick carefully to avoid damaging the brittle vines.

MELONS AND WINTER SQUASH These long-season crops that produce weighty fruits require heavy-duty support if you choose to grow them vertically, but it can certainly be done, and is a good space-saving option, if a little labor intensive. Larger varieties may even need slings made of cloth to support the fruit. You'll also need to tie the vines to the support using strips of cloth; avoid string or wire, which can cut into the vines.

13

CREATE YOUR OWN AMERICAN POTAGER

A potager is a French kitchen garden that is packed with a colorful mix of vegetables, fruits, herbs, and flowers. As beautiful as it is useful, a potager helps you eat more healthfully because fresh food is just steps from your back door. Herbs offer flavor without calories. And edible flowers sprinkled into salads and soups give home-prepped meals a fine-restaurant flair. Here are some tips for creating the ultimate (and beautiful) kitchen garden:

PLANT CLOSE TO YOUR HOUSE
Locate the kitchen garden where you can view it from indoors and where you're likely to walk past it every day. You'll be more likely to weed, water, and harvest–and you'll easy see what's ready to pick.

ENCLOSE THE GARDEN A kitchen garden should be a separate place–an oasis of food, flavor, and fragrance. In some situations, fences or walls might be practical for keeping out animals; in others, hedging or a line of trees simply suggests a sense of enclosure.

INCORPORATE STRUCTURE Consider adding architectural elements, such as planters that contain clipped boxwood balls or an

espaliered fruit tree. A bamboo trellis in the middle of a raised bed not only provides an architectural detail but also a leg up for climbing beans, peas, and other vines. In colder climates, the kitchen garden structure will offer beauty during winter when it is covered in snow rather than in peas.

PLANT EDIBLES WITH ORNAMENTALS Vegetables and flowers can stand shoulder to shoulder in the garden. You can create beautiful vignettes each season when you plant perennial edibles, such as asparagus, with perennial flowers, such as yarrow. This commonsense planting strategy clusters plants with similar sowing, maintenance, and harvesting needs in the same spot.

14

GROW COOL-WEATHER SALAD GREENS

One of the earliest types of plants in the garden to be harvested, spring greens offer a wild palette of flavors. Most grow quickly from seeds in the cool, moist weather of spring.

1. CURLY ENDIVE Bitter-flavored, it's best blended with other greens. The inner leaves are more mild; the outer leaves have a bite.

2. MÂCHÉ Also known as corn salad, it has a delicate nutty flavor. The leaves are good combined with mustard and delicious sautéed.

3. OAKLEAF Delicate flavor with tender leaves. Harvest it young or allow it to grow into a mature head.

4. ARUGULA Peppery flavor. Plant seeds every 10 days for continuous harvests.

5. BELGIAN ENDIVE A chicory with crunchy, slightly bitter leaves. Use raw in salads or stuff the slightly concave leaves.

6. BEET GREENS Leaves have an earthy taste like the root on which they grow. The plants are as ornamental as they are edible.

7. WATERCRESS Little leaves have tangy, peppery flavor. Grow in bogs or water gardens.

8. RADICCHIO Enlivens with color and slightly bitter notes. It's a tender perennial grown as an annual.

9. ESCAROLE Use its sturdy leaves in salads when they are young. Also good sautéed. If you'd like to blanch plants to improve flavor, withhold light for a week or two before harvest.

10. MIZUNA Its tender, peppery leaves are popular in Japanese cuisine. Cut leaves and stems as you need them; they will resprout.

11. FRISÉE Great texture with a bitter flavor. Add this frilly green to salads to give added texture and bite. Delicious with warm vinaigrette, bacon, and poached eggs.

15 KNOW YOUR COOL-WEATHER CROPS

Fill a raised bed, containers, or other landscape spots with these easy-to-grow favorites. Be sure to place smaller plants along sunny south edges.

MIXED LETTUCE Every 2 to 3 weeks, plant another crop of lettuce seeds or plants. Try a mix that includes 'Black Seeded Simpson', 'Red Sails', and romaine.

CARROTS Whether you eat them raw, sautéed, or cooked, this easy-to-grow root crop has a distinct, sweet flavor that will make you want to plant an extra row next year.

POTATOES While most people are familiar with the white-flesh Irish potato, there are many other varieties of this South American plant that offer red, blue, yellow, or bicolor flesh.

EARLY PEAS, THEN BEANS In early to midspring, plant peas along a trellis. Once the peas are finished, plant pole beans for a second crop.

BROCCOLI Famous for being packed with nutrients, broccoli is tasty and easy to grow. Plant it about a month before your area's average last spring frost date and in late summer for fall harvests.

CABBAGE Cabbages can be as ornamental as they are edible. Choose varieties called early cabbage for spring harvests. Late cabbage varieties are better for planting midsummer and harvesting in fall.

CHIVES Begin harvesting this perennial herb as soon as its new leaves appear in spring. The foliage has the classic chive flavor, but the late-spring blooms are edible too and taste more like onion.

SPINACH A so-called "super food" because it's packed with nutrients, spinach is a cinch to grow. Like other leafy greens, plant some in a shaded spot to keep harvests going into the summer months.

SWISS CHARD Colorful purple, pink, red, gold, orange, or white stalks carry glossy green heart- or arrow-shape leaves that taste a bit like spinach.

BRUSSELS SPROUTS Brussels sprout plants have trunklike stalks that grow 2 to 3 feet (60 to 90 cm) tall. Each stalk may produce up to 100 sprouts.

CAULIFLOWER Cauliflower is trickier to grow than its cousin broccoli. But harvesting a large, attractive head will give a great sense of satisfaction.

RADISHES Grow these fast-growing root vegetables from seed. Plant sequential crops for a continuous supply and interplant with lettuces or carrots.

DOUBLE UP ON POTATOES

There are two peak seasons for potatoes. Baby or new potatoes are planted in early spring and are harvested in mid- to late spring, before they reach full maturity. They have especially tender flesh.

Late-season potatoes are planted in midsummer and are harvested in the fall and early winter, when they are fully mature. Try these hybrids:

1 'Norland' This white-flesh potato stores well and is good for roasting and boiling.

2 'Kennebec' These thin-skin white-flesh potatoes are perfect for frying.

3 'Green Mountain' Similar to a russet, this heirloom variety has a floury texture.

4 'Adirondack Red' The moist and dense flesh of this waxy potato is red, unlike other red potatoes, which have white flesh.

5 'Adirondack Blue' This recently created hybrid has intensely hued flesh due to anthocyanins.

6 'Laratte' The satiny flesh of these fingerlings is exceptionally creamy when steamed.

7 'Keuka Gold' and 'Yukon Gold' The yellow flesh of these potatoes is a perfect balance of flouriness and waxiness.

8 'Red Golds' These waxy potatoes keep their shape when boiled—perfect for salads.

9 'Red Clouds' The flesh of these red-skin potatoes is uncommonly dry, making it an ideal boiling potato.

17

PLANT SOME SPUDS

This Peruvian native has been grown, harvested, and enjoyed in America since 1621. Known commonly as a spud, a potato is actually a tuber. Plant potatoes in compost-enriched soil and full sun. A site that receives 6 hours of sun daily will suffice.

STEP 1 Cut seed potatoes into pieces that include at least two eyes (sprouts) each. Let the pieces dry for several days before planting them.

STEP 2 Use a hoe or similar tool to make a furrow 5 inches (13 cm) deep. Plant seeds 12 inches (30 cm) apart and cover them with soil. Water the plantings regularly if nature doesn't do it for you.

STEP 3 When plants reach 1½ feet (45 cm) tall, hoe soil up around the plants to cover stems, leaving the top 4 inches (10 cm) of leaves exposed. Repeat when plants grow another 1½ feet (45 cm).

18

DIG INTO NEW POTATOES

SMALL VS. NEW Not all small red and white potatoes are new. The distinction goes to freshly harvested immature potatoes, which have a creamy, waxy texture and less starch than full-grown potatoes.

THIN-SKINNED Delicate skins mean you don't need to peel these little spuds. But do be gentle when you clean them–scrub too hard and you'll rub the skin right off.

STORE SMART Because of their thinner skin, new potatoes are more perishable than mature potatoes like russets and Yukon golds. Store them in a paper bag in a cool place and use within a few days of harvest.

19

UNBURY TASTY TREASURE

You can dig potatoes from mid- to late summer. The plants signal the end of their growth by turning yellow and withering. During hot weather, spuds store best in the ground, but all varieties should be harvested before the ground freezes.

STEP 1 Use a garden fork to loosen dry soil. Dig carefully along the perimeter of the planting areas to avoid spearing potatoes and damaging them.

STEP 2 Feel around in the loosened soil and pull out any potatoes. Large, deep-growing tubers may need more prodding with a trowel to wiggle them loose.

STEP 3 Rub potatoes between your hands to remove most of the soil that clings to them. Avoid rinsing potatoes before storing them; added moisture can promote

STEP 4 Before storing, spread the spuds on a flat surface in a cool (60°F to 75°F) (16°–24°C), dark, airy place for a week or two. Store spuds away from light to prevent them from turning green and developing toxic glycoalkaloids.

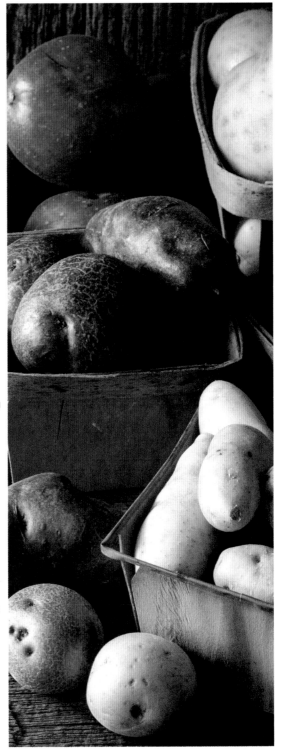

20

GROW TOMATOES FROM SEED

Tomato plants are classified either as indeterminate or determinate. Indeterminate plants grow all season, continuing to bloom and produce fruit as long as weather conditions are favorable. Determinate plants grow to a certain size, set fruit, and stop growing. Plant a combination of both.

Be sure to look at the "days to maturity" when you think about how to select tomatoes for your garden. If you live in a short-season climate, make sure you don't choose a tomato that takes 100 days to ripen –otherwise you may not get fruit before frost. Try these hybrids:

1 'Cloudy Day' hybrid, 70 days to maturity

2 'Brandy Boy' beefsteak hybrid, 75 to 78 days to maturity

3 'Baby Boomer' cherry hybrid, 50 to 55 days to maturity

4 'Big Mama' paste hybrid, 80 days to maturity

5 'Fourth of July' hybrid, 49 days to maturity

6 'Madame Marmande' hybrid, 72 days to maturity

7 'Cherry Baby' cherry hybrid, 67 to 70 days to maturity

8 'Supersteak' beefsteak hybrid, 80 days to maturity

9 'SuperSauce' hybrid, 70 days to maturity

21 KNOW YOUR HOT-WEATHER CROPS

Fill a raised bed, containers, or other landscape spots with these easy-to-grow favorites. Be sure to place smaller plants along sunny south edges.

PEPPERS Pepper plants are all the rage at garden centers. Try bell peppers in raised beds, purple-foliage ones in the landscape, and ornamental spicy ones in containers.

EGGPLANTS Eggplants are one of the most beautiful vegetables in your garden's landscape. Their fruits range from deep purple to striped to creamy white.

OKRA Some gardeners grow okra simply for its hibiscuslike blooms, but you can enjoy the vegetables at their peak by harvesting them at 2 inches (5 cm) long or shorter.

TOMATOES Patio tomatoes are ideal for novice gardeners. Grow them in containers and small gardens. Try cherry tomato plants for an abundance of bite-size fruits.

BASIL This tender annual takes off once the weather warms up. Use leaves fresh in salads, ground into pesto, and snipped into summer pasta.

ZUCCHINI Plant zucchini for its large tropical-looking leaves and prolific fruits. Harvest them at 6 inches (15 cm) long for optimum flavor.

GREEN BEANS Both types of green beans—bush beans and pole beans—can be planted every 2 weeks to give you harvests all summer.

CUCUMBERS Plant cucumber vines beside a trellis. Try a mix of classic slicing varieties, smaller pickling ones, and long Asian varieties.

CORN Plant early-, mid-, and late-season varieties to ensure the longest season of harvest. Choose from standard sugary (su), sugar-enhanced (se), and supersweet (sh2) varieties with yellow, white, or bicolor kernels.

ARTICHOKE The edible parts of this relative of the thistle are actually flower buds. The most highly desired part of the vegetable is the heart, positioned at the base of the bracts, below the hairy center.

MELONS Try honeydew, with a light green or orange flesh; casaba melon, with white flesh; and Crenshaw melon, with a pinkish flesh. All melons need extended temperatures above 70°F (21°C) to grow.

SWEET POTATOES Sweet potatoes require a long, warm growing season. Plant slips (sprouts) of sweet potatoes after spring weather has warmed and all danger of frost has passed.

22

KNOW WHAT TOMATOES CRAVE

Tiny tomatoes of all varieties can find a home in your garden. Cherry, grape, pear, and currant types are the candies of the tomato world,

SUN No getting around it: Sun is where it's at for tomatoes. Find a spot that gets at least 8 hours.

WARMTH As much as they love sun, tomatoes also love warm temps. Wait until your region gets to the air temp recommended on the label. Live in a super hot area?

Find a tomato specifically bred to withstand the heat.

NUTRIENTS Tomatoes are greedy eaters. Fertilizers can help. Mulch: Add a couple of inches around your plants. The weeds won't thank you, but the soil and the tomatoes will.

RIGHT AMOUNT OF WATER Drought is a tomato killer, hit-and-miss watering is a tomato killer, and too much water–same thing. Give them an inch a week, including rain.

AN EARLY DRINK It's better to water slow and deep than quick and fast. Water early in the day so the plants can get totally dry. (Wet leaves = pathway to disease.)

SUPPORT We're not talking the emotional kind. We mean physical support–a stake, a trellis, a cage. These are cheap and easy to find at a hardware store.

23

TASTE THE PAST: HEIRLOOMS

Most tomatoes do really well in large pots filled with a potting mix designed for container-grown plants. Just be sure you have a pot that's at least 12 inches (30 cm) in diameter; many tomato varieties can grow 6 feet (1.8 m) tall by the end of the season.

START Delay planting until frost is past. Ideal temps for growing and fruiting are 80s (F) (26°–31°C) during the day, 50s (F) (10°–15°C) or 60s (F) (16°–21°C) at night.

SUN A minimum of 8 hours per day.

SOIL Fertile, well-drained soil is a must. Improve both factors by spading in lots of organic matter before planting.

SUPPORT Plants can reach 10 feet (3 m) or more. Tie vines to a fence to keep these heavy producers from sprawling.

SUSTAIN Tomatoes need consistent food and water. As soon as fruits set, feed weekly with a balanced fertilizer.

24

RAISE IT UP

Raised-bed gardens are just that: gardens that have been lifted off the ground. Pretty simple, right? Just a little lift does plants a world of good, including:

LESS BENDING You'll save your back and knees with beds that are elevated above ground.

LONGER GROWING SEASON Because the bed is higher, it tends to get warmer more quickly in the spring for growing earlier and longer.

EASY ACCESS Access from both sides means you never have to step foot in the soil to weed, plant, or water.

MOISTURE CONTROL Because you're building up a garden bed, you can also escape too-wet or too-dry soil by filling yours with rich loam.

BETTER DRAINAGE Loamy soil means better-drained soil.

NO CREEPING CHARLIE It's harder for turf to spread into raised beds.

SAVE SPACE No space between rows equals more you can fill with plants.

THE BEST VEGGIES TO GROW IN RAISED BEDS

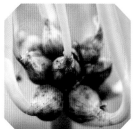

LEAFY GREENS Plant in early spring and early fall so you get two crops of these cooler-weather veggies.

TOMATOES Pick a compact variety to fit in to your smaller raised beds.

CARROTS Forgot to harvest these when the cold weather hit? No worries: This sturdy root veggie can overwinter in your raised bed.

ONIONS Harvest onions every couple weeks so as to get a range of sizes and flavor intensities.

25

HEAT UP WITH CHILE PEPPERS

Few plants grab the attention of eyes and taste buds like spicy chile peppers. A classic summer vegetable, these culinary staples are easy to grow, and they brighten gardens and plates with summery hues.

THE FAMILY TREE All peppers are the fruit of *Capsicum* plants. The term chile, in common usage, has come to refer to spicy types, but the essential difference between sweet peppers and hot chiles is the amount of capsaicinoids–the substances that give peppers their heat. For pepper enthusiasts, growing and eating the hottest chiles–the aptly named Carolina Reaper is the current heat champion–is a point of pride. Varieties with more modest heat still provide some zip but without overpowering other flavors.

GROWING BASICS Once established, pepper plants require moderate water and fertilizer. With full sun and plenty of warmth, chiles fruit prolifically all summer until frost. They languish in cool, damp conditions, so don't be in a hurry to get them in the ground in spring. Whether picked green or left to ripen on the plant or windowsill, peppers can be used raw, cooked, and preserved for long-term storage by drying or freezing.

WRINKLY SKIN
Healthy jalapeños sometimes exhibit "corking"—rough lines on the skin. It's natural, even prized by some.

26

PLANT PEPPER SEEDS

Start seeds indoors 12 to 16 weeks before planting out in late spring. It's easy to save your own pepper seeds, but plants readily cross-pollinate, so the offspring might not match the parent.

27

GROW YOUR OWN POPCORN

Popcorn from the store may taste fine, but popcorn from your own backyard tastes even better. Fresh popcorn kernels have an extra crunch and purity of flavor. Homegrown popcorn also provides extra-personal (and delicious) gifts for friends and relatives, especially when presented whole on the cob.

To grow your own 10×10-foot (3×3-m) patch of popcorn, you'll need at least 100 popcorn seeds, a sunny garden spot, well-draining soil, and warm temperatures. Corn likes a lot of hot sunshine and doesn't do well sitting in puddles. Plant once the danger of spring frost has passed. If your area is prone to raccoons, add a critterproof fence around your patch. Fencing also can block wind to help the 7-foot (2 m) popcorn plants stand tall despite their shallow root systems.

Popcorn can also be planted in containers, as long as the pots are at least 2 feet (61 cm) across. A line of large popcorn-planted pots along a sunny edge of a patio makes an interesting privacy wall.

TIP: Pop your own corn–directly on the cob! Simply remove the papery husks and place an ear of dried popcorn inside a brown paper lunch sack. Then insert another paper sack over the opening so corn is completely covered. Microwave on high 1 to 2 minutes or until the popping starts to slow down.

MATERIALS

Shovel or tiller

Fertilizer, such as aged manure

Hoe

Ruler or tape measure

Popcorn seeds

Rain gauge

STEP 1 Loosen the soil with either a shovel or tiller, working in aged manure or 12-12-12 organic fertilizer as you turn the soil.

STEP 2 Create a grid by carving small trenches or holes in the soil with your hoe. Space rows 1 foot (30 cm) apart. Place one seed every 1 foot (30 cm). Cover with 1 inch (2.5 cm) of soil; water with a gentle spray. If it's extremely hot, plant kernels a little deeper—up to 2 inches (5 cm) below the surface.

STEP 3 Give your plants 1 to 2 inches (2.5–5 cm) of water a week. You can measure water by using a rain gauge set in your garden. If rainfall is less than an inch, you'll need to supplement. After the popcorn sprouts, feed your seedlings with an organic fertilizer.

STEP 4 At the end of the growing season, the cornstalks will turn brown, and the kernels will begin to dry and get hard. When the ears of corn start to point downward, they are ready to pick. Twist each ear to separate it from the stalk. Make sure the popcorn kernels are completely dry by picking off a few kernels and tossing them into hot oil in a pan. If the popcorn is ready, it will pop. If it doesn't pop, lay the remaining corn in a single layer in a dry, protected space (such as a basement or garage) until hard.

28

RAISE VEGGIES IN CONTAINERS

Growing vegetables in containers is an easy way to experience the flavor and freshness of homegrown produce.

PICK A SUNNY SPOT

Most vegetables grown in a vegetable container garden do best in full sun (at least 6 hours of direct sun a day). Most vegetables aren't fussy about what kind of vegetable container they grow in. The only basic requirements are that it is large enough to hold the plant and that it has drainage holes so excess water can escape. Look for containers that are at least 10 inches (25 cm) wide and 12 inches (30 cm) deep. Large flowerpots, half barrels, plastic-lined bushel baskets, window boxes, planters, and large containers (5-gallon [19-L] buckets) work just fine. If your container does not have drainage holes, you will need to add several. Use a ¼-inch (6-mm) drill bit to create holes in the bottom or along the sides near the bottom.

Plants that grow tall or produce vines, such as tomatoes and cucumbers, will be more productive if grown up a support. A wire cage, inserted into the container at planting time, will do. Use large, heavy containers for trellised plants to minimize the risk of tipping.

USE GOOD SOIL

As is the case with most other types of container gardens, your vegetable container garden will do best in potting mixes made for containers. Ask at your nursery for a mix designed for use in large outdoor containers.

Or save money by blending your own vegetable container garden mix. Use equal parts of peat moss, potting soil, and vermiculite, perlite, or clean sand.

Plant container gardens the same time you would plant in the garden. Depending on what types of vegetable you want to grow, you can start seeds in your containers, grow transplants from seeds started indoors, or purchase transplants from a garden center.

WATER, FEED, AND INSPECT

Regardless of whether you are planting seeds or transplants, thoroughly water the container before you plant. Soak the potting mix completely, then allow it to sit for a few hours to drain excess water. Consistent watering is the key to container garden success. Inspect your vegetables regularly to make sure the potting mix hasn't dried out. Make watering your vegetable container garden easier by installing a drip-irrigation system. It can automatically irrigate your vegetables for you.

Starting about a month after planting, feed your vegetables about once a week with a water-soluble fertilizer, following the package directions. Also keep an eye out for weeds and other pests. Remove or treat any plants that show signs of disease or insect damage.

29

PLANT A GRILLSIDE KITCHEN GARDEN

Gardening season is also dining alfresco season. Planting a little herb garden in several containers brings the two together so that you can enjoy summer flowers and fresh herbs while you hang around the BBQ or patio table. A tall, potted kitchen garden offers herbs and edible flowers within clipping distance from your grill.

The materials could not be simpler to assemble. Tall ceramic chimney flue tiles are available in many sizes and shapes. They are hefty, sturdy, and resist tipping when planted.

They're also tall enough to hold plenty of soil for plants' roots, and drainage is not a problem because the tiles are open at both ends.

Find flue tiles at concrete companies, masonry shops, and builder supply stores that sell pavers and stone. If possible, go to the stoneyard yourself and check on the different sizes of tiles. Consider the dimensions of your grill area and choose several tiles that will make an attractive grouping. An odd number seems to look best, and several heights give the grill garden more interest and definition.

To add color, plant annual flowers that bloom all summer long alongside herbs to season grilled chicken, fish, burgers, and

vegetables. Once you get home with your flue tiles and plants, this garden will be ready for a party in about 20 minutes.

MATERIALS

Chimney flue tiles (an odd number in various shapes and sizes)

Protective gloves

Shredded-wood mulch

Potting soil

Fertilizer or compost, optional

Plants (a selection of edible flowers and herbs)

STEP 1 Set the flue tiles up on end around your grilling station. Large rectangular tiles are naturally suited to making a corner to define the space. Smaller tiles nestle comfortably in front of larger ones. Cluster the tiles together or use them to outline a larger space, setting one at each corner of a patio or positioning them as an inviting entrance to the area.

STEP 2 Wearing gloves, fill the largest tiles about halfway with wood mulch. Wood chips provide great drainage for the flue tiles and reduce the amount of potting soil needed to fill them. Over time, the wood breaks down and incorporates into the soil.

STEP 3 Fill the tiles with potting soil, mixing in organic fertilizer or compost if desired. Add the plants. Large tiles (up to 24 inches [60 cm] wide) easily hold two plants each. Water well and you're done. Add fresh potting soil every spring to top off the containers and replant as needed.

30
ASPIRE TO ASPARAGUS

Find a sunny spot for asparagus in your garden and you'll harvest this essential spring delicacy for years.

Growing your own asparagus is an investment of time and patience that pays off in tender, delicious spears of success. Plant the root crowns in well-drained soil in a sunny spot in your garden, give them a little attention while they become established, and you should be able to harvest a fine crop of asparagus every spring for 20 years or more.

It will always be the first crop in your garden–and the first few spears taste best right there by the bed, as soon as you pick them, on a cool spring morning. The harvest period lasts for up to 8 weeks; if the first half-dozen spears don't make it all the way to the kitchen, you'll still have plenty of time to experiment with recipes.

Asparagus, of course, is a perennial plant. It is possible to grow asparagus from seed, but most gardeners start with 1- or 2-year-old plants (available at garden shops and through mail-order specialists); they have long white roots that look like tassels, spreading down from

a central crown. Popular modern varieties hybridized in the breeding program at Rutgers University in New Jersey are all Jersey boys: 'Jersey Knight', 'Jersey Giant', 'Jersey Supreme', and others are all-male plants, developed for high yield, thick and uniform stalks, and superior disease resistance. You can still find old-time varieties, such as 'Martha Washington', but they are neither as productive nor as trouble-free as modern hybrids. Older varieties also typically include female plants, which produce bright-red berries but are not desirable because the berries

ripen and drop seeds; the seedlings eventually crowd asparagus beds, making them difficult to manage.

Plant asparagus crowns in spring. The planting area should be accessible from all sides; planting along a fence is not a good idea because keeping weeds out of an asparagus bed is crucial. If you can't reach the planting area easily, weeds will creep in. Dig a trench measuring about 6 inches (15 cm) deep and 1 foot (30 cm) wide. Make mounds of compost and soil in the trench about 18 inches (46 cm) apart and set a crown on each mound, fanning the roots around the mound, with the top of the crown about 3 inches (8 cm) below the original soil line. Fill in to just cover the crowns and water well. If you are planting more than one row, make the rows at least 1 foot (30 cm) and up to 5 feet (1.5 m) apart: You will need to walk between the rows to harvest your crop.

As the shoots emerge, add soil gradually until the soil level in the row is level with the surrounding soil. Then cover well with compost.

The year you plant, do not harvest any spears. They will grow to ferny foliage that helps increase the size and vigor of the crowns.

The second spring, take a few spears, but no more than six from each plant. Each spear should be thicker than a pencil. The third year, you should be able to harvest asparagus for 2 to 3 weeks. Cut or break the spears off at soil level when they are 8 to 10 inches (20–25 cm) tall and while the tips of the spears are still nice and tight. Harvest until the emerging spears are quite thin, then stop for the season and let the tall, ferny fronds develop.

Asparagus beetles inevitably find their way to asparagus plants. They eat the foliage, which weakens the plants and makes them susceptible to disease. Control the beetles with insecticidal soap or plant buckwheat or sunflowers nearby to attract beneficial insects, including ladybugs, that eat the beetles and their larvae. Above all, keep your asparagus bed weeded. Weeds compete with asparagus plants for moisture and nutrients and crowd your crop. Weeding assiduously helps you reach your goal of harvesting more spears than you could ever bother to count.

ASPARAGUS BASICS

It's time to plant. Nurture asparagus plants while they are becoming established for years of delicious spring harvests.

STEP 1 Plant crowns in a sunny place, in well-drained soil enriched with compost. Dig a trench up to about 1 foot (30 cm) deep and 1 foot (30 cm) wide.

STEP 2 Set the crowns on mounds of soil in the trench. You'll need 25 root crowns for a family of four asparagus enthusiasts; 50 would be even better.

STEP 3 Cover the crowns themselves with soil, but do not fill the trench. You'll be filling it gradually throughout the season. Firm the soil around the crowns; water well.

STEP 4 Spears are ready to harvest when they are about 8 inches (20 cm) tall. In a mature asparagus bed, you'll be able to pick fresh asparagus nearly every day.

STEP 5 Cut off spears (or break them) at soil level. If you use a knife, be careful not to cut too low; you could damage the crowns of the plants.

STEP 6 Asparagus foliage grows 6 feet (1.8 m) tall or more. Leave it on the plants until late fall or winter, then cut the stems back to about 2-inch (5-cm) stubs.

WATCH FOR PESTS
Common asparagus beetles lay dark eggs that seem to stand on end along asparagus spears. If you see them, pick them off and drop them in soapy water.

Hatched beetles will eat spears and foliage, weakening plants; in a small asparagus patch, control beetles by picking them off your plants.

31

DISCOVER MICROGREENS

The seeds of vegetables, salad greens, herbs, and edible flowers produce delicious young stems and leaves for harvesting–by snipping the stems–after only 2 or 3 weeks of growing. If left to grow, microgreens become young seedlings, then full-fledged plants. Unlike sprouts (germinated seeds that are eaten roots and all), microgreens need potting mix and bright light to grow.

One of the freshest forms of nutritious produce is also one of the easiest crops for a sunny windowsill. Start with a single crop–the easiest ones are radish, kale, Swiss chard, broccoli, and mizuna. Or sow a mix of seeds with similar maturity rates and harvest a combination of colors, textures, and flavors at once.

SEEDS

Sow microgreens from seed. A packet typically produces one or two crops in a 3-inch (7.6-cm) pot. Bulk seeds, most often sold in ¼-, 1-, 5-, or 25-pound (113-g, 454-g, 2.3-kg, or 11.3-kg) packages are more economical for larger crops.

CONTAINERS

Indoors, grow microgreens in a 3- to 4-inch-deep (7.6–10 cm) container with excellent drainage. Three-inch peat pots fit on a windowsill and group readily in nursery flats. Plastic produce boxes, take-out food trays, and nursery flats also work well. If the container doesn't have drainage, poke a few holes in its bottom using an awl or knife tip.

LIGHT, AIR, AND WATER

Grow microgreens indoors in the bright light of a south-facing window. If stems appear weak and pale, provide supplemental light using a shop light with two fluorescent bulbs: one cool and one warm lightbulb or full-spectrum bulbs. Place the bulbs 2 or 3 inches (5–8 cm) above the seedling tops.

Adequate ventilation also helps microgreens grow strong and healthy. A small desk fan improves air circulation.

Grow microgreens in a sterile, soilless mix and water carefully. Too much causes seeds and seedlings to rot; too little and crops fail. When the medium begins to feel more dry than damp, remoisten it. Water by soaking the containers' bottoms in a tray or saucer of water. Watering the tender plants from above often causes their stems to collapse and rot.

HARVEST

Microgreens will be ready for harvest at different stages of growth, from the appearance of cotelydon (the earliest, winglike seed leaves) to the first sets of true leaves. Most greens grow 1 to 3 inches (2.5–7.6 cm) tall. Once harvested, the plants will not grow back.

Ensure microgreens' quality by cutting them at the optimal time– early morning or evening–and keep them cool and fresh until use.

32 GROW MICROGREENS INDOORS

Among the easiest and fastest-growing crops possible, microgreens offer a range of fresh flavors, from mild to spicy, and inspire repeated plantings for an ongoing supply of tasty greens for creative uses.

STEP 1 Round up the materials you will need to sow the seeds of microgreens: 3-inch (8-cm) peat pots (or other suitable containers), potting mix, vermiculite, seeds, plant labels, and plastic wrap.

STEP 2 Premoisten the soilless seed-starting mix, a sterile medium that is formulated to promote seed development. Sprinkle warm water onto the mix and blend until it is thoroughly damp.

STEP 3 Fill each container with premoistened seed-starting mix—no need to pack it into place. Set the container on a watertight drip tray or saucer.

STEP 4 Sprinkle seeds evenly over the surface of the seed-starting mix, sowing them more thickly than you ordinarily would. Leave at least a seed's-width of space between the seeds.

STEP 5 Cover the seeds with vermiculite. This mineral-based material absorbs water and releases it slowly, keeping seeds damp but not too wet. Follow instructions for planting depth provided on the seed packet. Some seeds should be barely covered; others need thicker covering to germinate (sprout and grow) well. Label plantings.

STEP 6 Water the sown seeds with a gentle shower, soaking the vermiculite without washing away the seeds. Until the seeds germinate and green shoots sprout from them, water lightly as needed to keep the seed-starting mix damp. If the mix is too wet, seeds can rot and fail to grow.

STEP 7 Cover the containers with a lightweight sheet of plastic or a domed lid to maintain humidity and promote germination. Set the drip tray on a heat mat designed for seed starting or on a heating pad set on medium.

STEP 8 When the seeds germinate, remove the lid and the heat source. Set the containers on a sunny windowsill. Keep the planting medium damp and promote healthy growth by watering from the bottom: Pour water into the tray and allow it to be absorbed into the soilless mix.

33 SWEETEN YOUR LIFE: PLANT FRUIT

Fruit comes from different types of plants: vines, shrubs, canes, and trees. Try this selection of easy fruits for homesteads.

BLUEBERRY An ideal plant for the edible landscape, these low-growing or tall woody plants can be used as a hedge or colorful shrubs in a foundation planting or mixed border.

BRAMBLES A small patch of brambles—blackberries and raspberries—will easily provide enough berries for a family of four for fresh eating, baking, making jams, and freezing.

GOOSEBERRY Gooseberries are hardy fruiting shrubs that grow well in cool, humid regions of North America. They grow well in partial shade and produce large crops of tart fruit.

FIG Even if the fig plant freezes to the ground in winter, it often recovers, bearing fruit the following summer. The silvery branches of the fig plant also add drama to the landscape.

PEACH A perfectly ripe peach says summer. Among the smallest deciduous fruit trees,. pruned standard-size trees are easily maintained at12 to 16 feet (3.7–4.6 m) tall.

PEAR Planting a pear tree in your yard produces bushels of juicy ripe fruit.. Pears are easy to grow where spring is warm and dry and are beautiful in all seasons.

STRAWBERRY Growing about 6 inches (15 cm) high, strawberry plants produce white flowers in spring. followed by red berries in early summer or throughout the summer.

PLUM No stone fruit is more varied in origin, size, color, and flavor. Plum trees can be kept relatively small, growing 12 to 15 feet (3.7–4.6 m) tall if pruned annually.

CHERRY Whether you like them sweet or sour, cherries are beautiful fruit trees. One or two trees provide a large-enough crop for plenty of fresh eating as well as preserves.

APRICOT Fast-growing and small, one apricot tree produces more than 100 pounds (45 kg) of fruit in moderate climates. New cultivars make it possible to have fruit in cool climates too.

AVOCADO When grown in a moderate to tropical climate, full sun, and well-drained soil, an avocado tree will produce an abundant harvest of rich, buttery fruit. Leathery foliage provides year-round shade.

LIME Long-lasting plants produce juicy, sweet or tart fruit. In addition, lime trees have glossy evergreen foliage and fragrant flowers.

34

GROW YOUR OWN APPLES

There are more than 7,000 apple varieties. Your local cooperative extension service or garden center can help you choose ones that excel in your region. All apples do best in full sun and moist, well-drained soil. Although the trees thrive in a wide variety of soils, avoid planting them in low or wet spots.

Plant apples anytime from spring to fall. Dig a hole twice as wide as (but no deeper than) the pot your apple tree comes in. Remove the tree from the pot, loosen its root ball, and spread the roots so they face outward. Fill the hole with the soil you dug out and water the tree well.

PAIR UP FOR POLLINATION

Apples bear best when there are two varieties nearby to pollinate each other. Some apples have to be pollinated by another variety in order to bear fruit, so take note when you select varieties.

GROW APPLES IN CONTAINERS

Use large containers (at least 4 to 5 feet [1.2–1.5 m] in diameter) and choose dwarf varieties, which won't become too large for the pots. Fill pots with high-quality potting mix.

In warmer climates, leave pots outdoors all year. In colder climates, move trees to a protected spot such as an unheated garage or storage shed for the winter.

Keep container-grown apple trees watered well. Fertilize apples with a general-purpose timed-release plant food each spring.

GO ORGANIC

The perfect apples you see at the grocery may have been chemically treated. If you choose to grow apples organically, which means that you won't use chemical sprays, your trees will produce edible fruit, but you should be willing to tolerate a few superficial blemishes.

HARVEST TIME

There are early-, mid-, and late-maturing apple varieties, so the harvest season can stretch from August to October. If you plant a range with varying maturity, you'll enjoy the longest harvests.

Pick apples from the tree when they separate easily from the branch and have firm flesh. Soft apples are overripe, but can be used for cooking. Store them in a cool spot (under 40°F [4°C]) after harvest.

35

GROW TALL: COLUMNAR APPLES FOR SMALL SPACES

TALL AND NARROW Columnar apples grow straight up, 8- to-10-feet (2.4–3 m) tall, but only 2 feet (61 cm) wide. Also called urban apples, they're perfect for a compact garden or patio container.

LESS PRUNING The trees are easy to manage because they maintain themselves in the columnar shape, which means less pruning than standard apple trees.

FULL-SIZE FRUIT Although columnar apple trees are narrow, their fruit is full size.

A CHOICE OF FLAVORS Columnar apples come in a wide range of types and colors. Try Northpole, Blushing Delight, Golden Treat, Tangy Green, and Tasty Red.

A LIVING FENCE Line up a row of columnar apple trees to create a hedge row or living fence of fruit. Space trees 2 feet (61 cm) apart.

APPLE ALLEE Line a driveway or pathway with columnar apples to create a fruit-full allee.

SEASONAL COLOR Apple trees offer flowers in spring, fruit in summer and fall, and yellow leaves in autumn.

PLANT AT LEAST TWO Columnar apple trees, like regular apple trees, require cross-pollination, so plant two or more.

36

TAKE YOUR PICK: CIDER APPLES

Nothing compares to the taste of crisp fall apples pressed into cider. Mix tart with sweet apples to create custom cider blends. The more varieties the better. Single varieties make wonderful apple cider too.

On average, three medium apples equals a pound, and one pound (450 g) yields about a half-cup (118 ml) of cider. You'll need a half bushel or more of apples to make a gallon or two (4 to 8 L) of cider. You don't have to use an apple press; a juicer will work just fine. Here are some of the classic cider apples:

1. VIRGINIA HEWES CRAB A famous Southern cider apple with light green fruit, striped red at maturity, and a deep, layered flavor, both spicy and rich. Thomas Jefferson grew Hewes Crab at Monticello.

2. MOTHER From Massachusetts, about 1840, and once widely grown in England. The flavor has been described as almost pearlike, juicy with a sharp sweetness.

3. ROXBURY RUSSET A tart, spicy cider apple from the 17th century, the oldest American cultivated apple variety. One of its alternate names is Leather Coat.

4. HORSE A large round apple, probably from North Carolina in the late 18th century. Trees bear a heavy crop of tender, tart fruit. The green skin sometimes has a red blush.

5. GRIMES GOLDEN Said to have been discovered in what had been the former orchard of John Chapman (Johnny Appleseed) in West Virginia in 1804. Spicy, sweet, and sharp-tasting.

6. RHODE ISLAND GREENING From Rhode Island, probably around 1650. Crisp, tart fruits were very popular in Colonial times up through the early 20th century.

7. HARRISON This variety was thought to be lost, but it was rediscovered in 1989. The apples produce dark juice with complex, concentrated apple flavor touched with ginger and spice.

8. COX'S ORANGE PIPPIN Especially well-known for its fragrance. From England, around 1830.

9. RIBSTON PIPPIN A parent of Cox's Orange Pippin, from the late 18th century around Yorkshire, England. Ripens early. The fruit is juicy, firm, and very tart.

10. PITMASTON PINEAPPLE Small golden apples are sweet, a little nutty, and sharp-tasting, with just a hint of pineapple. From the 1780s.

11. BURFORD REDFLESH A Virginia apple, possibly a seedling of a crabapple, with medium to large fruit. This juicy, tart apple has speckled red skin and red flesh, which lend color to cider.

12. GOLDEN HARVEY A small golden apple from England, perhaps dating to the 1600s. It is aromatic, sweet, and sharply acidic. Sometimes called the Brandy apple.

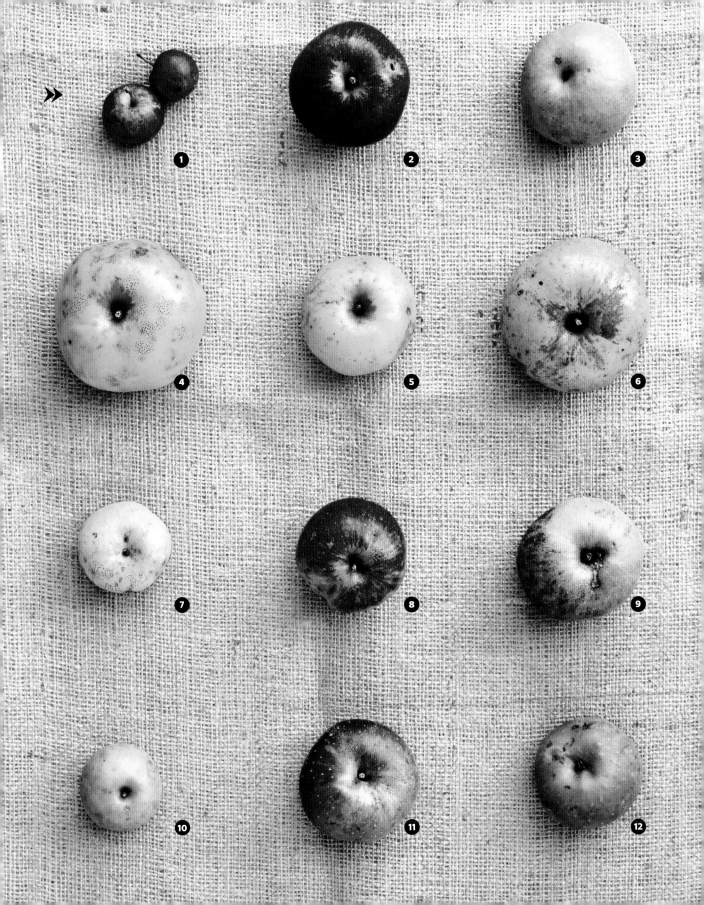

CHAPTER 2

Bees, Birds & Butterflies

A big part of the fun of living in the country is enjoying the range of creatures that visit your home. The winged species bring a particular kind of delight–and some of them, the pollinators, provide a very important function. Pollination is one of Mother Nature's ways to remind us that every creature great and small has a role to play in our world. Busy bees, indeed: More than one-third of the world's crops (as well as three-fourths of the world's flowering plants) depend on pollinators in order to reproduce. So plant with pollinators in mind: nectar-rich flowers, host plants, and natives.

37

FEED POLLINATORS

By planting a pollinator garden, you can help wildlife thrive while creating a beautiful spot on your property to enjoy nature.

Single flowers that face up, like Gaillardia 'Arizona Sun', are butterfly favorites.

38

GET THE BUZZ

Sustain bees, butterflies, moths, and other beneficial bugs in your backyard. Here's how to provide a pollinator-friendly garden.

FOOD Plant a spring-through-fall succession of sun-loving natives that offer a nonstop source of nectar and pollen. (For a month-by-month list of natives in your region, go to pollinator.org/guides.) Skip double-flowered hybrids–the meager nectar they offer is hard to reach. Plant shrubs and trees, such as dogwood, blueberry, and plum, that bloom in early spring when food is scarce. Include foliage host plants for larvae, including milkweed, parsley, fennel, and dill. Some pollinators are picky, relying on specific plants for survival. Monarch caterpillars, for example, eat only milkweed (*Asclepias*).

DISPLAY Advertise your menu by massing several of each species into drifts instead of polka-dotting singles throughout a border. From a bug's view, a big clump is like a leisurely sit-down restaurant. Butterflies and moths prefer landing on flat-face flowers; bees and flies like to investigate tubular flowers. A range of colors, shapes, and scents will attract the greatest diversity.

HABITAT Insects, particularly butterflies, hydrate by "puddling" (drinking from mud), so create a small wet spot in the garden or tuck in a birdbath. Most native bees are ground nesters, but some–notably the hardworking masonry bee–are cavity dwellers. Provide breakfast and a bed with a mason bee house. All pollinators give a five-star rating to unkempt gardens. Let their preference be your excuse to lower the bar on cleanup. Delay fall chores until spring–larvae overwinter in leaves, hollow plant stems, and branches.

DO NO HARM Avoid pesticides, including neonicotinoid insecticides, which have been implicated in the die-off of honeybees.

39

MEET THE POLLINATORS

Show some love to these industrious insects that carry a sweet burden for us.

NATIVE BEES More than 4,000 species, including the bumblebee, mason bee, and leafcutter bee. Each has a specialized pollinating job. Unlike social honeybees, most native bees are solitary, nesting in the ground or in holes.

HONEYBEES These hive dwellers were imported from Europe in the early 1600s to pollinate crops, including fruits, vegetables, and nuts. We rely on them for honey, too. Attracted to white, yellow, and blue flowers of all shapes and sizes.

MOTHS Moths take over at dusk for the night shift while the rest are napping. Geometer moths, hummingbird moths, hawk moths, and many others search for fragrant night bloomers in white or pale colors that reflect moonlight.

BUTTERFLIES Monarch, swallowtail, fritillary, painted lady, sulphur—the list goes on. Bees work more efficiently, but these leisurely flutterers turn food-driven flights into an aerial art form, landing on bright red, orange, yellow, and purple flowers.

FLIES Not the common housefly we swat, but a respectable society of gentle bee mimics, including hoverfly, flower fly, and midge. They go for the less glamorous flowers that others pass by. Stripes fool people and predators.

40

PLANT THE RIGHT HABITAT

THINK LOCAL A good native-seed company will have a special pollinator mix appropriate for your site–all native, specific to sun or shade conditions, and wet, mesic (moderately dry), or dry sites.

PLANT IN THE FALL A dormant seeding after the first hard freeze in the fall is the best time to plant pollinator habitat. That way the seeds will not germinate and grow that fall. Cold temperatures and winter precipitation settle the seed into the soil.

DON'T SKIMP ON SEED Seed can be expensive, but don't skimp if you want a good stand of prairie habitat. You only have to plant it once. Include at least 40 species of wildflowers and grasses.

MIX IN GRASSES Grasses keep the flowers from getting too tall and flopping over. If you plant in the spring, use a one-to-one mix of seeds per square foot (.09 m) basis. If planting in the fall, double the amount of grasses in the mix.

PREPARE YOUR SITE This may include mowing, chemicals, and fire. Here is your best chance to eliminate the weed competition to make room for your new baby plants.

OFFER PLANT DIVERSITY Some bees and most caterpillars are picky eaters –only feeding on certain types of plants. So the more plant diversity you offer, the more likely you will

support a wide variety of pollinators.

DESIGN FOR YOUR SPACE A mix of seeds will make your garden look more wild or prairielike. Consider how tall the plants will get. Some native plants grow to 8 feet (2.4 m); others are much shorter.

GO NATIVE Native seeds are easy to plant because they do not need to be in the soil. Simply scatter the seeds on bare soil and press them down firmly (walking on them works).

MANAGE WEEDS Perennial weeds need to be taken care of early using a variety of methods. In the first year, use a mower for large areas or hand-pull weeds so they don't shade out shorter prairie plants. Keep the ground sunny. Fire can

control certain invasives if your plot is large. A herbicide may be the only way to control some weeds.

MOW CAREFULLY Mowing suppresses the annual weed seedlings that choke out prairie plants the first year. By the second year, they should be able to handle the fight. Mow frequently the first year to 4 to 6 inches (10–15 cm). In the second year, mow once early in the year.

DO NOT DISTURB Once established, avoid disturbing more than one-third of the habitat any given year to protect the pollinators using it for nesting or feeding.

TAKE THE LONG VIEW Add more varieties of host and nectar plants each year.

ATTRACT POLLINATORS

Fragrance and color are nature's invitations to dinner. These flowers give the best "come hither" signals to pollinators.

BLANKET FLOWER Thanks to the "billboard" effect of its colorful petals, the blanket flower ranks in the top three favorites for a wide diversity of native bee species.

JOE PYE WEED A nectar source is critical in late summer, when butterflies are flying in hordes. A single plant keeps all sorts busy: hairstreaks, monarchs, swallowtails, and painted ladies.

SUNFLOWER Researchers have found that seed production on sunflowers is reduced without pollinators. Native bees work in tandem with honeybees to boost crops.

ASTER Asters attract a range of pollinators. Studies show that two-tone asters snag more visitors. Grow asters with yellow central disks amid petals of a different color.

PURPLE CONEFLOWER Squadrons of bees and butterflies visit this member of the daisy family. Check out the colorful new varieties of coneflower on the market.

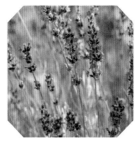

LAVENDER Although lavender attracts all manner of bees, honeybees are the most efficient pollinators of this perfume plant.

BUTTERFLY WEED For monarchs, milkweeds keep the next generation coming by furnishing food for the caterpillars that hatch from eggs laid on the plant.

BEE BALM As the name implies, bee balm attracts bees. Butterflies also love to alight on the liplike petals. Bee balm has a long blooming season, from mid- to late summer.

ROSEMARY Rosemary (*Rosmarinus officinalis*) offers blue blossoms and fragrant foliage that pollinators, especially bees, find irresistible. In warmer regions, this herb will grow into a sizable shrub.

COSMOS New varieties of cosmos begin blooming virtually the moment you set them in the ground and keep blooming until a hard fall frost. This nonstop source of pollen can be a boon for bugs of all descriptions.

RUSSIAN SAGE The plentiful wands of blue-blossom Russian sage (*Perovskia* spp.) serve as an important nectar source late in the season when other perennials are finished blooming.

HYSSOP Hyssop (*Agastache* spp.) opens the first of its flower-packed spires in spring and keeps performing until heavy frost. The orange, pink, or purple tubular flowers draw all kinds of beneficial bugs.

42

GET A START IN BEEKEEPING

Thinking about raising honeybees? Here's what you need to do.

LEARN ABOUT BEES Invest time in learning about the world of bees. Join a local beekeepers club or find a mentor.

SELECT A SITE Look for an out-of-the-way location with distance from neighbors, livestock, and public spaces.

A southeastern-facing spot with morning sun, afternoon shade, wind protection, and nearby nectar sources is best.

PURCHASE SUPPLIES You'll need a hive, supers (boxes for honey storage), a smoker (to calm bees when working the hive), a hive tool (to remove frames and supers from the hive), a bee veil (to protect your face and neck when working the hive), and gloves. Check farm supply stores, online suppliers, and local apiarists. Starter kits sell for U.S. $250 to $500.

CHOOSE BEES Talk with local beekeepers to find out the best types of bees for your area, then order stock for a spring delivery or pickup. While bees can be shipped, it's best to buy a "nuc" (nucleus hive, typically four or five frames with bees and brood) from a local apiarist.

HIVE THE BEES Late afternoon or early evening is the best time to hive the honeybees. Ask your supplier for detailed instructions. Check on the hive after a few days and begin following standard beekeeping practices.

43

WEAVE AN OLD-FASHIONED BEE SKEP

As far back as the 1600s, colonists carried honeybees to the New World to pollinate crops ferried from their homelands. Long before that, these humble structures developed to house honeybees graced the shores of the Nile, where Egyptian slaves tended cylindrical skeps constructed of baked clay. Similar clay skeps provided shelter for bees–and a source of domesticated honey–in ancient Greece. The woven basket-style skep first surfaced in ancient China and Ethiopia, and the bell-shape bee skep most familiar to gardeners today historically hosted beehives

in England, Belgium, Luxembourg, and West Africa.

Rye straw is ideal because it's the only grain mice won't eat. As long as it's kept dry, it lasts indefinitely. But you can use other local grasses, such as Harding grass. A skep is basically just grasses and a binding material, such as such as split blackberry, rattan cane, or linen thread, woven together like a basket.

Today, because bee keepers must be able to open their hives for inspection, it's impractical to keep bees in skeps.

But the art of the bee skep–the classic woven domed hive–is a throwback to days when this method of beekeeping flourished. While bee skeps are icons of the past, they also make beautiful modern garden

ornaments–and are both practical and beautiful. You can nestle a handwoven skep into a pollinator garden amid nectar-rich blooms or set one in the center of an herb garden as a focal point.

MAKE YOUR OWN BEE SKEP

STEP 1 Harvest rye straw using hedge clippers. Soak the 6-foot-long (1.8 m) straw for 3 hours in a copper rain gutter, similar to a trough from the 1700s.

STEP 2 Colonial skepmaking tools are simple: reed, linen thread, (here wrapped on a mother-of-pearl thread holder), spacing tool, and scissors.

STEP 3 Reed holds the rye coils together. Soak the reed in water for 10 minutes before using it. A colonial reproduction clothespin holds the coiled reed.

STEP 4 A skep begins at the center. Tie rye and reed with linen thread. The spacing tool creates openings between rye coils for inserting the reed, which holds coils tightly, side by side.

44

ENTICE BUTTERFLIES TO A WINDOW BOX BUFFET

Lure butterflies to your deck or patio if garden space is scarce. Flowering delicacies, including lantana, verbena, pentas, sanvitalia, globe amaranth, zinnia, marigold, calibrachoa, and gaura, keep winged diners coming back for nectar all season to this sunny windowsill. Many butterfly species will lay their eggs on curly parsley leaves, which provide an excellent source of food (host plant) for the larvae and caterpillars.

45

RESTORE NATIVE PLANT COMMUNITIES

When indigenous flowers and grasses grow freely among native trees and shrubs, they create a self-sustaining environment that supports plants and the resident birds, butterflies, bees, amphibians, and mammals that rely on them in every season. Native plants require less maintenance than exotic (nonnative) species because they are perfectly suited to the soil and climate.

Bees prefer flowers in blue, purple, and yellow. And they zero in on plants with a sweet fragrance. Natives include coneflowers and black-eyed Susans.

But be wary of invasive nonnatives, such as purple loosestrife, Japanese knotweed, crown vetch, and multiflora rose. Some adapt so well that they rampantly spread and bully native species into submission. Restore nature's balance by removing aggressive interlopers from your gardens and replacing them with bona fide native blooms.

46

BOOST BUTTERFLIES

Make even the smallest outdoor space a nectar mecca by planting any of the nectar-rich flowers featured here. You also can give a boost to butterfly populations by planting "host" plants to provide food for caterpillars. The common herbs parsley and dill, for example, are magnets for many species of egg-laying females. Adding even a few plants to host caterpillars can boost the numbers of butterflies in your yard by unbelievable numbers. Create these planters and you'll end up with a garden that's beautiful, satisfying, and–best of all–filled with more and more fascinating, colorful, and lovely fluttering wings.

1. Flat-leaf parsley *(Petroselinum crispum)* **2.** *Rudbeckia* 'Indian Summer' **3.** *Verbena bonariensis* **4.** *Echinacea purpurea* 'White Swan' **5.** *Hibiscus* 'Super Rose' **6.** *Sedum* 'Autumn Joy' **7.** Curly parsley *(Petroselinum crispum)*

1. *Buddleia* 'Honeycomb' **2.** *Rudbeckia* 'Toto Mix' **3.** *Buddleia davidii* **4.** 'Artist Rose' *Ageratum* **5.** 'Callie Orange' *Calibrachoa* **6.** *Buddleia davidii* 'Pink Delight' **7.** Aster 'Bouquet Powderpuff Mix'

47

CREATE A HUMMINGBIRD BUFFET

By planting a container of Salvia 'Mystic Spires' (*Salvia longispicata × farinacea*), Red and purple verbena (*Verbena canadensis*), Coral and raspberry autumn sage (*Salvia greggii*), you will attract hummingbirds all summer long.

48

CREATE A BUTTERFLY SIPPING STATION

Butterflies put in a lot of miles in an average day and need water, no matter how much nectar they drink. Construct a refreshing rest stop and they'll reward your kindness with their colorful, serene presence.

Make a butterfly-friendly watering station by filling a colorful ceramic bowl with a mix of sand and soil, then moistening the mix with water. Add a few shakes of table salt and tuck in a large flower, such as a Gerbera daisy, to catch butterflies' attention. Add decorative rocks in the center as perches for sipping visitors.

Butterflies look for places where water puddles, so leave the sipping station on the deck, patio, or garden's edge where it can fill with rainwater. Placing it in partial shade will slow the water's evaporation. Add water to the bowl as needed.

49

ATTRACT BIRDS

Make your balcony or yard a better place for birds and butterflies by including these:

PLACES TO HIDE Birdhouses are great, but so are trees and shrubs. Bonus: Trees and shrubs also shelter insects, which make great food for birds.

FOOD It's better for birds and butterflies if you plant a variety of blooms, berries, and seeds and a range of plant types–annuals, perennials, vines, grasses.

SUPPLEMENTAL FOOD Bird feeders–filled with different food such as black-oil sunflower, millet, and safflower–encourage a variety of birds to visit. If you start to fill feeders, don't stop–they come to depend on it. You also can try specialized options, such as hummingbird feeders.

SUN In general, butterflies feed only in the sun.

RESTING SPOTS Flat stones, perches in trees–both birds and butterflies need spots to snooze out of the reach of potential predators.

WATER Splash pools–even just a slim pan with an inch of water and a little sand–can be good spots for wildlife to bathe or get nutrients. Bonus points for a fountain that makes a wee bit of noise, a great attraction for birds and butterflies too.

NESTING SPOTS AND BOXES Trees, shrubs, and other sheltered areas as well as nesting boxes offer extra protection for birds.

50

MAKE A 5-MINUTE BIRDBATH

Create a splash with this easy birdbath made with two terra-cotta pots and one saucer. Use pots you have on hand or find new ones at a garden center. Add water and wait for winged friends to stop in for a drink or a splash.

Overturn and stack two different-size terra-cotta pots–a 12- and 16-inch-diameter (30-cm and 40-cm) pot work well for this project. Set the pots on the ground in the garden or place a 16-inch (40-cm) paver in the garden and set the pots on it for more stability. Set the saucer on top of the pots and fill it with water.

Empty the water from the birdbath every other day and clean the saucer before refilling it with fresh water.

Encourage the health of your winged visitors by scrubbing the birdbath regularly to help prevent the potential spread of disease caused by algae, bacteria, and bird excrement. Use a stiff brush to remove any debris from the saucer. Rinse thoroughly before refilling.

51

SAVE THE BEES

The Xerces Society for Invertebrate Conservation recommends these garden strategies for sustaining pollinator populations:

CREATE A POISON-FREE REFUGE Stop using pesticides and herbicides. (Acre for acre, the amount of chemicals poured onto residential lots exceeds that dumped onto agricultural fields.) Most broad-range pesticides don't discriminate. They smite the good bugs along with the bad. Target offenders with a safe alternative, such as an insecticidal soap spray.

PROVIDE SHELTER Pollinators need a protected place to live and reproduce. Leave some untended "wild" areas so they have undisturbed space to tend to business.

SERVE AN ONGOING BUFFET Native plants bloom at just the right times for local pollinators. Plant blocks of the same species to maximize a little bug's efficiency. Keep in mind that every butterfly was a caterpillar once and raise sacrificial plants for food purposes.

OFFER BEVERAGES TOO The moisture captured and stored in a boggy or muddy site gives insects something to drink when rainfall is scarce.

52

FEED THE BIRDS

Have fun with the harvest by turning seasonal bounty into family–and bird-friendly–projects. Share the fruits of autumn with your feathered friends. Make tasty treats from succulent slices of squash or pumpkin.

MAKE A SQUASH-RING BIRDFEEDER

MATERIALS

Half an acorn squash or
  small pumpkin
Knife
Peanut butter
Birdseed or raw, unsalted
  sunflower seeds
Raisins or other dried fruit
  bits (optional)
Small-gauge wire

STEP 1 Cut the acorn squash or small pumpkin into ¼- to ½-inch-thick (6–13 mm) circles. Smear one side with peanut butter.

STEP 2 Dip the peanut butter side of the squash into birdseed or sunflower seeds that are spread on a plate. If desired, add raisins or dried fruit.

STEP 3 Poke a wire through the squash circle. Twist the wire ends and hang the feeder high enough to be out of reach of neighborhood cats and dogs.

CHAPTER 3

Do–It–Yourself Recipes

If you're a homesteader, you're naturally a do-it-yourselfer–and what could be better than to make fresh, wholesome foods from scratch for yourself, family, and friends? Some of these recipes may be made entirely from what you grow or produce on your land. Some may require a little outside help. Either way, you'll know exactly what went into them–and the satisfaction of stocking your pantry with homemade foods is a large part of the reason you moved to the country, right?

53

BAKE KALE CHIPS

Preheat oven to 300°F (150°C). Thoroughly wash and drain 10 to 12 ounces (280–340 g) fresh green curly kale; pat dry with paper towels. Remove and discard the tough center stalks from leaves. Tear leaves into 2- to 3-inch (5–8 cm) pieces. In an extra-large bowl combine 1 tablespoon olive oil, ¼ teaspoon salt, and ¼ teaspoon smoked paprika. Add greens; toss to coat. Use your hands to gently rub the oil mixture onto the greens until thoroughly coated.

Place a wire rack on each of four baking sheets. Arrange greens in a single layer on the wire racks. Bake on separate oven racks about 20 minutes or until greens are crisp, rearranging baking sheets halfway through baking (if all four baking sheets won't fit in oven, bake in two batches). (For a dehydrator, place leaves in a single layer on mesh-lined dehydrator trays. Dehydrate at 135°F (57°C) 2½ to 3 hours or until dry and brittle.) Cool greens completely on wire racks before serving.

To store, transfer to an airtight container. Cover and seal. Store at room temperature 5 to 7 days. If the greens chips begin to lose their crispness, place them on a baking sheet and bake in a 325°F (160°C) oven 2 to 3 minutes.

54

GET JUICED

Drink this tomato juice blend straight up or add a splash of vodka to make a Bloody Mary.

PREP: 1 HOUR **COOK:** 35 MINUTES **PROCESS:** 35 MINUTES **MAKES:** 7 PINTS (7 250-ML JARS)

10	pounds (4.5 kg) tomatoes
⅓	cup (35 g) finely chopped celery
⅓	cup (50 g) finely chopped onion
⅓	cup (50 g) finely chopped carrot
⅓	cup (60 g) finely chopped red sweet pepper
1	tablespoon (18 g) salt
	Citric acid

STEP 1 Wash tomatoes. Remove stem ends and cores; coarsely chop tomatoes.

STEP 2 In an 8- or 10-quart (8- or 9-L) stainless-steel, enamel, or nonstick heavy pot combine tomatoes and the next four ingredients (through sweet pepper). Bring to boiling, stirring frequently; reduce heat. Simmer, covered, about 20 minutes or until tomatoes are soft, stirring frequently.

STEP 3 Press tomato mixture through a food mill or sieve to extract juice (you should have about 15 cups [3.5 L] juice). Discard solids. Return juice to the pot. Stir in salt. Bring to boiling; reduce heat. Simmer, uncovered, about 15 minutes or until desired consistency, stirring occasionally.

STEP 4 Add ¼ teaspoon (1.2 mL) citric acid to each of seven hot, sterilized pint canning jars. Ladle hot juice into jars, leaving a ¹⁄₂-inch (12 mm) headspace. Wipe jar rims; adjust lids and screw bands.

STEP 5 Process filled jars in a boiling-water canner 35 minutes (start timing when water returns to boiling). Remove jars from canner; cool on wire racks. (See #78).

HOT AND SPICY TOMATO JUICE BLEND Substitute finely chopped jalapeño, serrano, or other chile peppers (do not seed) for the red sweet pepper.

PER ½ CUP JUICE (125 ML), PLAIN OR VARIATION: 31 cal., 0 g fat, 0 mg chol., 259 mg sodium, 7 g carb., 2 g fiber, 1 g pro.

55

BREW KOMBUCHA

Enjoy this crisp, carbonated beverage for its refreshing flavor—and the probiotic benefits as well.

PREP: 20 MINUTES **COOL:** 1 HOUR **FERMENT:** 1 WEEK + 2 DAYS **MAKES:** ABOUT 16 SERVINGS

- **14** cups (3.3 L) water
- **1** cup (200 g) sugar
- **8** black tea bags
- **2** cups (500 ml) purchased plain kombucha, such as GT's Enlightened Kombucha brand
- **1** SCOBY* (tip, below)

STEP 1 Bring 4 cups (1 L) of the water to boiling. In a very large heatproof glass bowl or pitcher combine the boiling water and sugar; stir to dissolve. Add tea bags. Let stand 1 hour. Remove and discard tea bags. Add purchased kombucha. Transfer to a clean 1-gallon jar (3.8-L). Add SCOBY. Cover jar with paper towels and secure with a rubber band. Let ferment in a dark place where temperature is between 70°F to 75°F (21°–24°C) for 1 week.

STEP 2 Remove SCOBY with clean hands and store (tip, below. If desired, reserve enough kombucha (2 cups [475 ml]) to make another batch of kombucha. Strain remaining kombucha through a sieve lined with 100%-cotton cheesecloth; transfer to clean bottles with swing-top seals, leaving a 2-inch (5-cm) headspace. To carbonate, let stand in a dark place where temperature is between 70°F and 72°F (21°–22°C) 2 to 3 days. Chill before serving. Store kombucha in the refrigerator up to 1 month.

GINGER KOMBUCHA Prepare as directed through Step 1. Remove

SCOBY. Add 1 ounce (28 g) fresh ginger, peeled and thinly sliced, to the jar. Cover and chill 1 to 2 weeks. Remove and discard ginger. Continue with Step 2.

*TO MAKE A SCOBY In a large heatproof glass container combine 4 cups (1 L) boiling water and ½ cup (125 g) sugar; stir to dissolve. Add 4 black tea bags; let stand 1 hour. Remove and discard tea bags. Stir in 3 cups (750 ml) water. Transfer to a clean 2- to 3-quart (2–3 L) jar. Stir in 1 cup (250 ml) purchased plain kombucha. Cover jar with paper

towels and secure with a rubber band. Let stand in a dark place between 70°F to 75°F (21°–24°C) 3 weeks. Remove SCOBY with clean hands; discard liquid.

NOTE Kombucha is not meant to treat or cure any medical conditions. Drink no more than 8 ounces (250 ml) a day. Consult a doctor before use if you are pregnant, nursing, or have any health conditions.

PER 8 OUNCES (250 ML) DRINK, PLAIN OR VARIATION: 53 cal., 0 g fat, 0 mg chol., 10 mg sodium, 14 g carb., 0 g fiber, 0 g pro.

56
PREPARE PESTO

Some people like to squeeze lemon juice in their pesto to get a little more zip and to balance the fat of the olive oil and cheese. A tablespoon or two is all you need. Try it with and without to see which you prefer.

TOTAL TIME: 20 MIN.

- ⅓ cup (75 ml) olive oil
- 2 cups (50 g) firmly packed fresh basil leaves
- ½ cup (70 g) pine nuts, toasted
- 2–4 cloves garlic, peeled and coarsely chopped
- ¼ teaspoon (1.5 g) kosher salt
- 2 ounces (¾ cup [55 g]) Parmesan cheese, grated

  Olive oil

STEP 1 In a food processor combine the ⅓ cup (75 ml) olive oil, basil, nuts, garlic, and salt. Process until nearly smooth, stopping and scraping sides as necessary. Stir in Parmesan. Add enough olive oil to reach desired consistency. Makes 1 cup (250 ml).

STEP 2 To store, cover the surface of the pesto with plastic wrap (this keeps it from turning brown) and refrigerate up to 1 week.

PER 1 TABLESPOON PESTO: 85 cal, 8 g fat), 3 mg chol., 101 mg sodium, 1 g carb., 0 g fiber, 2 g pro.

Nuts release oils when toasted, making them even more flavorful. Cool completely before making your pesto or your sauce will be gummy.

Process, don't pulverize! Overprocessing results in bruised greens and a dull, lifeless sauce. Stop before the pesto is completely smooth—a few big flecks give it character.

You'll get significantly more flavor if you grate the cheese by hand. Because texture is key, stir it in after you've processed your other ingredients to avoid a thick, homogenous paste.

Everyone has a style of pesto they prefer (we like it thicker for smearing on sandwiches, thinner for pasta and veggies). Add olive oil as you wish for the consistency you like best.

57

TURN TOMATOES INTO KETCHUP

The bottled stuff can't compare to the fresh flavor of this spiced homemade ketchup. Time to make some french fries!

PREP: 1 HOUR **COOK:** 2 HOURS 15 MINUTES **PROCESS:** 15 MINUTES **MAKES:** 4 HALF-PINTS (4 250-ML JARS)

8	pounds (3.6 kg) ripe red tomatoes
½	cup (75 g) chopped onion
¼	teaspoon cayenne pepper
1	cup white vinegar (250 ml)
4	inches stick cinnamon, broken (10 cm)
1½	teaspoons whole cloves
1	teaspoon celery seeds
¾	cup sugar (170 g)
1	tablespoon salt

STEP 1 Quarter tomatoes; let stand in a large colander to drain. In an 8- to 10-quart (8–9 L) stainless-steel, enamel, or nonstick heavy pot combine tomatoes, onion, and cayenne pepper. Bring to boiling, stirring frequently; reduce heat. Simmer, covered, 15 minutes, stirring frequently.

STEP 2 In a small stainless-steel, enamel, or nonstick heavy saucepan combine the next four ingredients (through celery seeds). Bring to boiling; remove from heat. Cover and set aside.

STEP 3 Press tomato mixture through a food mill; discard skins and seeds. Return tomato mixture to the same pot. Stir in the sugar. Bring to boiling, stirring to dissolve sugar; reduce heat. Simmer, uncovered, 1½ to 2 hours or until reduced by half, stirring occasionally.

STEP 4 Strain vinegar mixture into tomato mixture through a fine-mesh sieve; discard spices. Stir in salt. Simmer, uncovered, 30 minutes or until desired consistency, stirring frequently.

STEP 5 Ladle hot ketchup into four hot sterilized half-pint canning jars, leaving a ½-inch (12 mm) headspace. Wipe jar rims; adjust lids and screw bands.

STEP 6 Process filled jars in a boiling-water canner 15 minutes (start timing when water returns

to boiling). Remove; cool on a wire rack. (See #78.)

TO FREEZE Prepare as directed through Step 4. Place pot in a sink filled with ice water; stir ketchup to cool. Ladle into half-pint freezer containers (250 ml), leaving a ½-inch (13 mm) headspace. Seal and label. Freeze up to 10 months. (See #88.)

PER 1 TABLESPOON KETCHUP: 21 cal., 0 g fat, 0 mg chol., 114 mg sodium, 5 g carb., 1 g fiber, 0 g pro

58

MAKE YOUR OWN MUSTARD

Fresh-ground mustard seeds have some heat! The pleasingly pungent flavor of this coarse-ground mustard will mellow as it sits.

PREP: 15 MINUTES **STAND:** 24 HOURS **CHILL:** 1 DAY **MAKES:** 1½ CUPS (375 ML)

- ⅔ cup (160 ml) white wine vinegar
- 5 tablespoons yellow mustard seeds
- 5 tablespoons brown mustard seeds
- ½ teaspoon salt
- ½ teaspoon ground ginger
- ⅛ teaspoon ground allspice
- 3 tablespoons honey
- 2 cloves garlic, minced

STEP 1 In a medium bowl combine the first six ingredients (through allspice). Cover and let stand at room temperature 24 hours (the seeds will absorb the liquid).

STEP 2 Add honey and garlic to mustard seed mixture. Transfer mixture to a blender or food processor. Cover and blend 1 to 2 minutes or until desired texture and consistency (mixture will not get completely smooth), stopping to scrape down sides as necessary.

STEP 3 Spoon mustard mixture into four 4-ounce (125 ml) canning jars or airtight storage containers. Chill 1 to 2 days before serving, for best flavor.

CRANBERRY MUSTARD Prepare as directed in Step 1, substituting red wine vinegar for white wine vinegar and stir ½ teaspoon cracked black pepper into the mustard seed mixture with the spices. Continue as directed in Step 2, but omit honey. In a small saucepan combine ½ cup (50 g) fresh cranberries and ⅓ cup (75 ml) pure maple syrup. Bring to boiling; reduce heat. Simmer, uncovered, 5 minutes or until berry skins pop. Add cranberry mixture to mixture before blending.

CREOLE MUSTARD Prepare as directed in Step 1, except stir ¼ teaspoon cayenne pepper into the mustard seed mixture with the spices. Continue as directed in Step 2, except reduce honey to 1 tablespoon and add 2 to 3 teaspoons prepared horseradish to mixture before blending.

TO STORE Store sealed jars in the refrigerator up to 3 months.

PER 1 TABLESPOON MUSTARD: 29 cal., 1 g fat (0 g sat. fat), 0 mg chol., 49 mg sodium, 3 g carb., 0 g fiber, 1 g pro.

59

HATCH HOMEMADE HOT SAUCE

Apple adds a touch of sweetness to this sriracha-style hot sauce.

PREP: 1 HOUR 15 MINUTES **FERMENT:** 3 DAYS **COOK:** 10 MINUTES **MAKES:** 9 CUPS (2 L)

- **3** quarts (3 L) bottled spring water
- **4½** tablespoons all-natural fine sea salt
- **3** pounds red chile peppers, such as Fresno, stemmed and quartered (1.25 kg) (tip, #85)
- **2** pounds (1 kg) red apples, cored and cut into chunks
- **1** head garlic, cloves separated, peeled, and coarsely chopped
- **¼** cup (50 g) sugar
- **¼** cup (60 ml) cider vinegar

STEP 1 In a 6-quart (6 L) ceramic crock or glass container combine the water and salt; stir to dissolve. Add chiles, apples, and garlic. Place a plate that fits just inside the container on the chile mixture to keep it submerged. Cover container with a kitchen towel. Ferment at room temperature (70°F to 75°F) (21°–24°C) 3 to 5 days or until bubbles form around the edges, skimming off any white residue that forms on the surface.

STEP 2 Using a slotted spoon, transfer chiles, apples, and garlic to a 6- to 8-quart (6–7.5-L) stainless-steel, enamel, or nonstick pot. Add 6 cups (1.5 L) of the liquid. Stir in sugar and vinegar. Bring to boiling, stirring occasionally; reduce heat. Simmer, covered, 10 minutes or until apples are tender.* Using an immersion blender, blend mixture until smooth. (Or cool slightly and process in batches in a blender until smooth.)

STEP 3 Firmly press mixture through a fine-mesh sieve into a bowl (the more solids that are pressed into the liquid, the thicker the sauce will be). Discard solids remaining in sieve. If desired, return strained mixture to pot and boil gently, uncovered, 10 minutes or until desired consistency.

Transfer sauce to clean jars or bottles; seal and label. Store hot sauce in the refrigerator up to 6 months.

RECIPE NOTE The process of blending and boiling the mixture will produce strong vapors, so be sure you have proper ventilation before you begin.

PER 1 TEASPOON SAUCE: 3 cal., 0 g fat, 0 mg chol., 69 mg sodium, 1 g carb., 0 g fiber, 0 g pro.

DRESS A SALAD WITH VINAIGRETTE

Head to your herb garden to make this classic vinaigrette—and then to the lettuce patch for some fresh greens with which to toss it.

PREP: 20 MINUTES **COOL:** 1 HOUR **FERMENT:** 1 WEEK + 2 DAYS **MAKES:** ABOUT 16 SERVINGS

1	cup olive oil (250 ml)
⅓	cup red wine vinegar (75 ml)
¼	cup finely chopped shallots (25 g)
2	tablespoons snipped fresh oregano, basil, thyme, and/or parsley
1	tablespoon Dijon-style mustard
2 to 3	teaspoons sugar
2	cloves garlic, minced
	Salt and black pepper

STEP 1 In a screw-top jar combine the first seven ingredients (through garlic). Cover and shake well. Season to taste with salt and pepper. Serve immediately or cover and store in the refrigerator up to 3 days. (The olive oil will solidify when chilled, so let vinaigrette stand at room temperature 1 hour before using.) Stir or shake well before using.

GREEN ONION · DILL · HERB · ASIAN GINGER

GREEN ONION VINAIGRETTE Roughly chop the white and green portions of 16 green onions. In a blender combine chopped green onions; 1 cup (250 ml) olive oil; ½ cup (125 ml) lemon juice; 2 tablespoons white wine vinegar; 2 tablespoons honey; 2 tablespoons snipped fresh basil, thyme, or parsley; 1 tablespoon Dijon-style mustard; and 2 teaspoons ground coriander. Cover and blend until smooth. Season with salt and pepper.

DILL VINAIGRETTE In a blender combine ½ cup (125 ml) canola oil; ½ cup (125 ml) olive oil; ⅓ cup (75 ml) tarragon vinegar or white wine vinegar; ¼ cup (25 g) finely chopped shallots; 2 tablespoons snipped fresh dill; 1 tablespoon Dijon-style mustard; 2 to 3 teaspoons sugar; 2 cloves garlic, minced; and ¼ to ½ teaspoons hot pepper sauce. Cover and blend until smooth. Season with salt and pepper.

ASIAN GINGER VINAIGRETTE In a screw-top jar combine 1 cup (250 ml) canola oil; ¼ cup white wine vinegar (60 ml); 2 tablespoons snipped fresh basil, thyme, and/or parsley; 2 to 3 teaspoons sugar; 2 cloves garlic, minced; ¼ cup (60 ml) soy sauce; 1 small fresh jalapeño pepper, seeded and finely chopped (tip, #85); 1 tablespoon finely chopped pickled ginger; 1 tablespoon liquid from the jar of pickled ginger; 1 tablespoon lime juice; and 1 tablespoon toasted sesame oil. Cover and shake well. Season to taste with salt and pepper.

PER 2 TABLESPOONS DRESSING, PLAIN OR VARIATIONS: 143 cal., 15 g fat (2 g sat. fat), 0 mg chol., 47 mg sodium, 1 g carb., 0 g fiber, 0 g pro.

61

CHURN YOUR OWN BUTTER

Home-churned butter is so easy to make—and it's a really fun thing to do with kids. After you've churned your own butter, try a flavored butter (see #62).

START TO FINISH: 10 MINUTES **MAKES:** 1⅔ CUPS (300 G)

1 quart (1 L) whipping cream*

½ teaspoon sea salt or kosher salt (optional)

STEP 1 Place the cream in the bowl of a stand mixer. Using the whisk attachment, beat the cream on medium-high about 8 minutes or until the fat and liquid separate. (Place a towel over the mixer to avoid getting splashed toward the end of mixing.)

STEP 2 Line a large sieve with a double layer of 100%-cotton cheesecloth and set it over a bowl. Pour the mixture through the sieve. Gather the cheesecloth around the butter and squeeze to get as much of the liquid out as possible. (Reserve buttermilk for another use.)

STEP 3 If desired, place butter in a medium bowl and use a rubber spatula to knead in salt. Pat butter with a paper towel to remove any excess liquid. Transfer the butter to a piece of parchment paper or waxed paper. Form into a log or square, wrap, and chill until ready to use or up to 2 weeks.

*RECIPE NOTE If using ultra-pasteurized whipping cream, it may take longer to beat before the butter separates from the liquid (about 12 minutes total).

PER 1 TABLESPOON BUTTER: 102 cal., 12 g fat (7 g sat. fat), 31 mg chol., 2 mg sodium, 0 g carb., 0 g fiber, 0 g pro.

Beat the cream on medium-high speed. Hold a towel around the bowl to minimize spattering, especially when the butter and buttermilk separate.

Transfer the buttermilk and butter to a cheesecloth-lined sieve. Use a rubber scraper to remove the butter from the whisk attachment.

Pull the edges of the cheesecloth up around the butter and squeeze out as much of the buttermilk as possible.

62

FLAVOR YOUR BUTTER

In a large mixing bowl beat butter with a mixer on medium until light and fluffy, scraping bowl occasionally. Add desired stir-in. Beat on low until combined. Divide flavored butter among four pieces of plastic wrap or waxed paper. Shape each portion into a 4-inch (10 cm) log. Wrap each log in plastic wrap, then in foil. Chill up to 2 weeks or freeze up to 3 months.

BLACKBERRY-HONEY BUTTER In a food processor combine 1/2 cup (70 g) fresh blackberries and 1/2 cup (125 ml) honey. Cover and process until smooth. Strain through a fine-mesh sieve, discarding seeds. Stir in 1/2 cup (70 g) additional fresh blackberries, coarsely chopped.

CILANTRO-LIME BUTTER In a small bowl stir together 1/3 cup (15 g) finely snipped fresh cilantro, 2 tablespoons finely chopped fresh jalapeño chile peppers (tip, #85), and 1 tablespoon finely shredded lime peel.

DILL-CHIVE BUTTER In a small bowl combine 2 tablespoons finely snipped dill, 2 Tbsp. finely snipped chives, and 1 teaspoon freshly ground black pepper.

GREMOLATA BUTTER In a small bowl stir together 1/3 cup (10 g) finely snipped fresh Italian parsley, 2 teaspoons finely shredded lemon peel, and 2 cloves garlic, minced.

RASPBERRY BUTTER In a small bowl mash together 1 cup (125 g) fresh raspberries and 2 tablespoons powdered sugar.

TARRAGON-SHALLOT BUTTER In a small bowl stir together 1/4 cup (5 g) finely snipped fresh tarragon and 2 tablespoons finely chopped shallot.

CULTURE YOGURT

There's not a bit of sugar or gelatin (common ingredients in store-bought brands) in this yogurt.

PREP: 30 MINUTES **SLOW COOK:** 5 MINUTES (HIGH) + 5 MINUTES (HIGH) PER HOUR OF STAND TIME
STAND: 4 HOURS **CHILL:** 4 HOURS **MAKES:** 4 PINTS (2 LITERS)

8 cups (2 L) whole milk*

¼ cup (60 ml) plain unsweetened yogurt containing active yogurt cultures, at room temperature

STEP 1 In a 4-quart (4 L) saucepan heat milk over medium heat until an instant-read thermometer inserted in milk registers 180°F to 185°F (82°–85°C), stirring frequently. Remove from heat. Let stand at room temperature until thermometer registers 110°F to 113°F (43°–45°C), stirring before checking temperature. (Cool milk more quickly by placing saucepan in ice water for a few minutes.)

STEP 2 In a small bowl stir together 1 cup (250 ml) of the warm milk and the unsweetened yogurt, whisking until smooth. While stirring constantly, slowly pour the milk-yogurt mixture back into the milk in saucepan. Ladle mixture into four clean 1-pint (500-ml) canning jars, leaving a 1-inch (2.5-cm) headspace. Adjust lids and screw bands.

STEP 3 Place filled jars in a 6-quart (6-L) slow cooker. Pour enough lukewarm water (about 108°F) (42°C) into the cooker to reach just over halfway up sides of jars. Cover cooker and cook on high 5 minutes. Turn off cooker, wrap cooker with a thick towel, and let stand about 4 hours or until yogurt is thick, turning on cooker to high for 5 minutes every hour.

STEP 4 Remove jars from cooker. Chill 4 hours or until yogurt is set. Store, tightly covered, in the refrigerator up to 2 weeks. If desired, reserve some of the yogurt as a starter for a future batch.

FLAVORED YOGURT Before adding the yogurt to the cooled milk mixture in Step 2, stir in 1 tablespoon vanilla or instant espresso coffee powder.

FRUITED YOGURT Before chilling the yogurt, stir 2 tablespoons mashed ripe fruit (such as blueberries, raspberries, peach, or mango) into each jar.

*RECIPE NOTE For low-fat yogurt, substitute low-fat milk for the whole milk.

PER ½ CUP (125 ML) YOGURT, PLAIN OR VARIATIONS: 84 cal., 4 g fat (2 g sat. fat), 13 mg chol., 67 mg sodium, 7 g carb., 0 g fiber, 5 g pro.

BAKE ARTISAN BREAD

This no-knead artisan bread has a crisp crust and a tender crumb. Try it toasted and slathered with home-churned butter (#61) and homemade strawberry jam (#81).

PREP: 25 MINUTES **CHILL:** 4 HOURS **STAND:** 35 MINUTES **RISE:** 1 HOUR
BAKE: 25 MINUTES AT 400°F (200°C) **MAKES:** 12 TO 16 SLICES

- ¾ cup (175 ml) warm water (105°F to 115°F [40°–46°C])
- 1 package (8 g) active dry yeast
- ½ cup (125 ml) milk
- 2 tablespoons sugar
- 2 tablespoons butter or olive oil
- 1½ teaspoons salt
- 2¾ cups (350 g) all-purpose flour
  Nonstick cooking spray or olive oil
  Cornmeal
- 1 egg, lightly beaten
- 2 teaspoons water

STEP 1 In a large bowl stir together the ¾ cup (175 ml) water and the yeast; let stand 5 minutes. Meanwhile, in a small saucepan heat and stir the next four ingredients (through salt) just until warm (120°F to 130°F [49°–54°C]) and butter, if using, almost melts. Stir milk mixture into yeast mixture until combined. Stir in flour (dough will be sticky). Lightly coat a medium bowl with cooking spray or brush with oil; transfer dough to the greased bowl. Lightly coat a sheet of plastic wrap with cooking spray or brush with oil; cover dough with greased plastic wrap, coated side down. Refrigerate 4 to 24 hours.

STEP 2 Using a dough scraper or spatula, carefully loosen dough from bowl and turn out onto a floured surface. Cover with greased plastic wrap. Let stand 30 minutes.

STEP 3 Grease a baking sheet; sprinkle lightly with cornmeal. Gently shape dough into a 6-inch (15-cm) round loaf, lightly flouring dough as needed. Transfer to prepared baking sheet, using dough scraper or spatula if necessary. Cover and let rise in a warm place until nearly double in size (1 hour).

STEP 4 Preheat oven to 400°F (200°C). Combine the remaining ingredients; brush over loaf. Bake 25 minutes or until a thermometer registers at least 200°F (93°C). If necessary to prevent overbrowning, cover with foil the last 5 minutes. Remove; cool on a wire rack.

PER SLICE: 199 cal., 7 g fat (3 g sat. fat), 29 mg chol., 469 mg sodium, 27 g carb., 2 g fiber, 7 g pro.

65

MAKE FRESH MOZZARELLA

Fresh mozzarella—like all fresh cheeses—is not aged and is easy to make at home. The flavor is fresh and sweet. Try some with ripe garden tomatoes and basil or on a fresh tomato pizza (#66).

PREP: 40 MINUTES   **STAND:** 10 MINUTES   **COOL:** 20 MINUTES   **MAKES:** 12 OUNCES (340 G)

1¼ cups (300 ml) cool unchlorinated (filtered) water (about 55°F [13°C])

1½ teaspoons citric acid*

1 gallon (3.8 L) whole milk, preferably from a local dairy (do not use ultra-pasteurized milk)**

¼ teaspoon liquid rennet or ¼ of a rennet tablet*

1½ teaspoons sea salt

STEP 1 In a Dutch oven or large pot combine 1 cup of the cool water (250 ml) and the citric acid, stirring to dissolve citric acid. Stir in milk. Heat over medium heat until an instant-read thermometer inserted into the milk mixture registers 88°F (31°C), stirring frequently. This is barely warm to the touch, so it doesn't take long to heat. (If your milk gets slightly hotter than this, remove from the heat and let it cool to 88°F [31°C].)

STEP 2 Remove milk from heat. In a small bowl stir together the remaining ¼ cup (60 ml) cool water and the rennet. Add rennet mixture to milk mixture, stirring 30 seconds. Let stand 10 to 15 minutes or until the curd looks like custard and is soft-set (curd will be cream color and fairly smooth with liquid around it).

STEP 3 With a knife that is long enough to touch the bottom of the pan, cut curd in a grid pattern into approximately 1-inch (2.5-cm) squares. The curd should hold a cut edge (if it doesn't, let it stand longer). Line a colander with 100%-cotton cheesecloth; set colander in a bowl. Ladle curds into colander. Drain off most of the whey. (If desired, reserve the whey for another use.) Transfer the curds to a large glass bowl. Some of the whey may remain in curd.

STEP 4 Microwave curds, uncovered, 45 seconds (this works best if your microwave has a turntable). The mixture should start to develop curds and look a bit like cottage cheese at this point. Transfer curds to a fine-mesh sieve to drain off whey. Return curds to glass bowl. Stir in salt. Stir with a spoon or knead with your hands to work it into small pieces and squeeze the curds about 1 minute.

STEP 5 Microwave 30 seconds more; drain and knead curds again. Repeat microwaving and kneading one to three more times as needed to get the cheese to start to flow like taffy and be shiny when kneaded (the temperature of the cheese should be about 135°F [57°C] in order for this to happen). The cheese will be hot, so wear one or two layers of clean rubber gloves when handling it. Knead and stretch gently a few times, just until shiny and smooth. Form into a ball, tucking ends under to make it as smooth as possible on top.

(If desired, you can form several smaller balls.) At this point, the curd will easily hold a ball shape and most of the whey will be drained off. If the cheese cools and feels rubbery and hard to shape while kneading, place it back in the bowl and microwave 15 to 20 seconds to soften. Place the ball(s) of mozzarella in a bowl of ice water.

STEP 6 Cool cheese completely in ice water (about 20 minutes). It is now ready to eat. (Or store it in water in the refrigerator up to 5 days, changing the water daily. Or drain it and wrap the cheese in plastic wrap, then refrigerate.)

*KITCHEN TIP Citric acid makes the cheese stretchy, and rennet coagulates the milk to form curds. Look for citric acid at health food and specialty food stores and at pharmacies. Find tablet or liquid rennet at specialty food stores or in the pudding or gelatin section of your grocery store.

**NOTE Some milk is too ultra-pasteurized to form curds. Use milk from a local dairy that is not ultra-pasteurized. Organic milk may be ultra-pasteurized, so read the label. You can also use low-fat milk, but the cheese may not have quite the same texture or richness.

PER 1 OUNCE (25 G) CHEESE: 218 cal., 11 g fat (7 g sat. fat), 35 mg chol., 489 mg sodium, 17 g carb., 0 g fiber, 11 g pro.

66

TOP A TOMATO PIZZA

Place a 15×10×1-inch baking pan (40×25×2-cm) on the lowest rack of the oven. Preheat oven to 475°F (240°C).

For sauce, in a food processor combine 2 cups (300 g) cherry tomatoes, 1 tablespoon olive oil, 1 sprig fresh oregano, and 1 clove sliced garlic. Process just until tomatoes are coarsely chopped (do not puree). Set sauce aside.

Lightly sprinkle all-purpose flour on an 18-inch-long (46 cm) piece of parchment paper. On the paper roll one 1-pound (450 g) ball fresh room-temperature pizza dough into a 14×8-inch (36×20-cm) rectangle. Spread the sauce over the dough, leaving a 2-inch (5-cm) border around the edges.

Carefully remove preheated pan from the oven. Place pizza (still on parchment) into the pan and return to the lowest rack of the oven. Bake 10 minutes. Top with 8 ounces (225 g) fresh mozzarella cheese sliced 1/4-inch thick (6 mm). Bake 5 minutes more or until pizza is crisp on the bottom. Sprinkle with 1/4 teaspoon sea salt. If desired, top with 1 cup (30 g) baby arugula and 2 ounces (60 g) very thinly sliced prosciutto, cut into strips.

CHEW ON HOMEMADE JERKY

You'll need a dehydrator to make this maple-cracked pepper jerky. If you don't have one, consider getting one: It's a useful tool to have as a DIYer for dehydrating fruits, vegetables, and herbs.

PREP: 20 MINUTES **STAND:** 10 MINUTES **MARINATE:** 1 HOUR **DEHYDRATE:** 5 HOURS **MAKES:** 13 OUNCES (370 G)

- **2** pounds (1 kg) boneless beef chuck roast and/or boneless beef sirloin roast*
- **1** cup (250 ml) reduced-sodium soy sauce
- **2** tablespoons pure maple syrup
- **2** tablespoons. olive oil
- **4** cloves garlic, minced
- **2** teaspoons cracked assorted peppercorns or black peppercorns
- **2** teaspoons sea salt
- **1** teaspoon dried thyme, crushed

STEP 1 Place a steamer insert in an extra-large skillet. Add enough water to the skillet to come just below the steamer insert. Bring the water to boiling. Place roast in steamer insert. Cover; steam 10 to 15 minutes or until an instant-read thermometer inserted into the center of the roast registers 160°F (70°C). Place the roast on a cutting board and let stand 10 minutes.*

STEP 2 Using a sharp knife, trim excess fat from meat. Cut meat across the grain into ⅛- to ¼-inch slices (3- to 6-mm) that are 5 to 6 inches (13 to 15 cm) long.

STEP 3 For marinade, in a large bowl combine the remaining ingredients. Add meat to marinade, stirring with a fork to coat the meat evenly. Cover and marinate in the refrigerator 1 to 2 hours. (The longer you marinate, the stronger the

flavor.) Drain meat in a colander; discard marinade.

STEP 4 Place meat slices in a single layer on mesh-lined dehydrator trays.

STEP 5 Dehydrate at 160°F (70°C) 5 to 6 hours or until dry. To check doneness, remove one slice from dehydrator; the slice should easily break in half when bent if done. Let cool. Cooled jerky can be kept in an airtight storage container

at room temperature for up to 3 weeks.

*KITCHEN TIP: To make it easier to slice the meat thinly for jerky, freeze the meat 10 to 30 minutes to firm it up.

PER 1 OUNCE (25 G) JERKY: 87 cal., 4 g fat (2 g sat. fat), 39 mg chol., 255 mg sodium, 1 g carb., 0 g fiber, 12 g pro.

68

MAKE SOME BACON

This black pepper-brown sugar bacon is amazing and surprisingly simple to cure yourself.

PREP: 30 MINUTES **CHILL:** 6 DAYS + OVERNIGHT **SMOKE:** 1 HOUR 30 MINUTES **MAKES:** 5 POUNDS (2.25 KG)

- ⅓ cup (65 g) brown sugar
- ¼ cup (70 g) coarse kosher salt
- 1 tablespoon coarsely ground black pepper
- ¾ teaspoon pink curing salt* (optional)
- 1 7- to 7½-pound (3- to 3.5-kg) slab pork belly,** rind removed

STEP 1 In a small bowl combine brown sugar, kosher salt, pepper, and pink curing salt (if using). Halve the pork belly crosswise and place each piece in a large resealable plastic bag. Add half of the sugar-salt mixture to each and rub it evenly into both sides of the pork belly.

STEP 2 Seal the bags, squeezing out all the air. Set the bags in shallow pans and refrigerate at least 5 days or up to 7 days, turning the bag once a day. (Liquid will begin to gather in the bag.)

STEP 3 Rinse cured pork belly with cool water. Pat dry with paper towels. Set a rack over a shallow baking pan. Place the cured pork belly onto the rack, fat side up, and refrigerate, uncovered, at least 24 hours or up to 36 hours to dry.

STEP 4 Prepare a smoker according to the manufacturer's instructions. Smoke the cured pork belly, fat side up, at 225°F to 250°F (110°–120°C) 1½ to 2 hours or until it reaches an internal temperature of 150°F (65°C). (Or for unsmoked bacon, preheat oven to 225°F [110°C].) Roast the pork belly, fat side up, on a rack set over

a shallow baking pan 1¾ to 2 hours or until it reaches an internal temperature of 150°F (65°C). Cool slightly. Cover and refrigerate bacon overnight until well chilled.

STEP 5 To serve, thinly slice desired amount. Cook slices in a large skillet over medium heat 8 to 10 minutes or until browned and crisp, turning to brown evenly. Store unsliced bacon in the refrigerator up to 3 weeks or freeze up to 3 months.

*KITCHEN TIP Pink curing salt contains a mixture of table salt and sodium nitrite. It preserves the pink color of the meat and aids in the prevention of botulism. Without it, the cured meat will become slightly gray in color. Look for pink salt at specialty cooking and food stores or from online sources.

PER 1 OUNCE (25 G) BACON: 168 cal., 16 g fat (6 g sat. fat), 23 mg chol., 94 mg sodium, 0 g carb., 0 g fiber, 3 g pro.

69

FERMENT SAUERKRAUT

There are just four ingredients in homemade sauerkraut: cabbage, pickling salt, sugar—and time.

PREP: 45 MINUTES **STAND:** 10 MINUTES + 2 HOURS **FERMENT:** 3 WEEKS **MAKES:** ABOUT 8 CUPS (1.2 KG)

3 to 4 pounds (1.5 to 2 kg) green or red cabbage

1½ tablespoons pickling salt

1 tablespoon sugar

STEP 1 Remove outer leaves from cabbage. Quarter cabbage heads lengthwise; remove cores. Using a mandoline, food processor, or large chef's knife, finely shred cabbage. Measure 2½ pounds (1.25 kg) shredded cabbage.

STEP 2 Place the 2½ pounds (1.25 kg) shredded cabbage in a large ceramic crock (such as the liner of a slow cooker), glass container, or plastic food container that holds at least 1 gallon (3.8 L). Add pickling salt and sugar. Using very clean hands or tongs, toss cabbage with pickling salt and sugar. Let stand 10 minutes. Using a clean, heavy plate that fits just inside the container, press plate down on cabbage. Let stand at room temperature 2 to 24 hours, tossing cabbage and pressing plate down on cabbage every hour or until enough liquid is released to cover cabbage by at least 1 inch (2.5 cm). (If cabbage does not release enough liquid, add enough water to cover in a ratio of 1 cup water [250 ml] to 1 teaspoon pickling salt.)

STEP 3 Place a large resealable plastic bag filled with 1 quart (1 L) water plus 4 teaspoons salt (or a clean 1-gallon jug [3.8 L] full of water) over the plate to weight it down. Cover container with a clean dishcloth or loose-fitting lid. Place container in a cool place out of direct sunlight to ferment. At temperatures between 70°F and 75°F (20°–24°C), fermentation will take 3 to 4 weeks; at 60°F to 65°F (15°–18°C), fermentation will take 5 to 6 weeks. The sauerkraut is ready when it has a slightly crunchy texture and pleasantly tangy flavor.

STEP 4 Every 2 or 3 days, replace dishcloth with a clean dishcloth, skim off any scum that forms on surface of cabbage, and clean and replace plate. If any discolored cabbage appears at the top, remove and discard it. If the water level gets too low, add enough water to cover in a ratio of 1 cup (250 ml) water to 1 teaspoon salt.

STEP 5 Transfer undrained sauerkraut to canning jars or airtight containers; seal and label. Store in the refrigerator up to 2 months.

PER ¼ CUP (150 G) DRAINED SAUERKRAUT: 10 cal., 0 g fat, 0 mg chol., 338 mg sodium, 2 g carb., 1 g fiber, 0 g pro.

Using a large knife, cut the cabbage into wedges. Remove and discard the cores, then thinly slice the wedges into shreds.

Combine shredded cabbage with pickling salt, crushing the cabbage with your hands to help the salt draw the water out of the cabbage.

Use a dinner plate to pack down the cabbage, pressing the plate down every hour to release as much liquid as possible.

Weight down the cabbage with a brine-filled plastic bag, allowing the liquid to rise above the cabbage and around the edges of the plate and bag.

CHAPTER 4

Canning & Freezing

Few sights are as satisfying as a pantry shelf lined with glistening jars full of vegetables and fruits you canned yourself. In addition to the emotional reward, canning and preserving your own food offers other benefits–such as fresh flavor, healthfulness, and economy. "Putting up" your own food is a great way to cut your grocery bills–especially if you grow your own produce. After the initial outlay for equipment, every gorgeous jar of food costs just pennies. Great abundance is created with very little in terms of dollars. Here's how to save the bounty of your garden (or CSA or farmers market) for another day.

70

STORE IT RIGHT

Whichever food preservation method you choose, be sure to store the final product correctly to ensure safety and preserve flavor. Keep canned food in a cool, dry place without sunlight. Store frozen foods at 0°F (–18°C) or below.

71

LEARN THE BASICS OF CANNING

Follow these basic rules to ensure success:

KNOW WHICH CANNER TO USE The boiling-water canner–basically a big pot with a lid and a rack in the bottom–is used for high-acid foods, which naturally resist bacteria growth. Pressure canners are used with low-acid foods and recipes that are prone to harboring harmful microorganisms. They heat food hotter than boiling-water canners. Recipes specify which type of canner to use. (See #72 for more information.)

CHOOSE THE RIGHT JARS Use jars made specifically for canning. Don't use glass jars from purchased food, even if they look like canning jars. Don't use jars that look different from the canning jars currently on the market. And avoid jars with chipped edges; that can affect the seal. Use the size jar specified in the recipe because it takes longer to achieve the critical internal temperature in larger jars. (See #77 for more information.)

USE LIDS PROPERLY Use the special two-piece lids manufactured for canning. Reuse the rings, but do not reuse the lids, which have a special sticky compound that seals the jar. Don't screw lids on too tightly or they won't create a vacuum seal. Heat the lids in

very hot but not boiling water or the compound won't seal (check the manufacturer's directions for preparing lids). Test for sealing on each jar after it has cooled. Press the center of the lid. If the button is depressed and does not make a popping sound, it has sealed properly. Remove and clean the rings before storing canned food.

CHOOSE THE RIGHT RECIPE Always use tested recipes from reliable, current sources–and follow the recipes exactly. Don't alter ingredients. Alterations can change the acidity and compromise food safety. (See #73 for more information.)

KEEP IT CLEAN AND KEEP IT HOT Keep everything scrupulously clean. Wash and sterilize jars. Pack hot food into hot jars one at a time– not assembly-line style. (See #77 for more information on how to sterilize jars and equipment.)

LABEL JARS WITH CONTENTS AND DATE Include a batch number if you can more than one load in a day (if a jar spoils, you can identify others from the same batch).

72

PICK A METHOD OF PRESERVATION

The way you process produce depends on the desired result. Should raspberries be made into a rich jam or simply frozen? Should the cucumbers be pickled and processed in a water canner or allowed to ferment?

BOILING-WATER CANNING
A boiling-water canner is a very large pot with a rack in the bottom and a lid. Jars are submerged in simmering water for a specified time. They are heated to a temperature of 212°F (100°C). This method is mainly for fruits, pickles, salsa, and other high-acid foods. It's also used for some tomato recipes.

PRESSURE CANNING
A pressure canner has a lid that locks onto the pot and a dial- or weighted-gauge that allows you to regulate the steam pressure that builds up inside the pot by turning the burner heat up or down. The pressurized steam is much hotter than boiling water–pressure canning heats jars to 240°F (116°C). This higher heat kills tougher microorganisms that can thrive in low-acid foods, such as green beans, corn, soups, and sauces with meat.

FREEZING
An easy way to preserve garden produce, freezing preserves texture in a way canning doesn't. Freezing is easy. Some fruits and vegetables require blanching before packaging, but for others, you can just put the food into airtight containers or bags and stash them in the freezer!

73

KNOW YOUR HIGH-ACID AND LOW-ACID FOODS

Foods for canning are divided into two groups: high-acid and low-acid.

HIGH-ACID FOODS These are the simplest to process. Their high acidity levels create a difficult environment for microorganisms and enzymes to thrive, so processing them in the lower heat of a boiling-water canner is safe.

High-acid foods have a pH of 4.6 or lower. Nearly all fruits, jams, and jellies are high-acid foods. Lemon juice, lime juice, and vinegar are very acidic. For that reason, most pickles and most salsas are high-acid, even though they may contain foods that are otherwise low-acid, such as green beans and carrots.

LOW-ACID FOODS These foods have a pH greater than 4.6. Most vegetables are low-acid, as are most soups, stews, and meat sauces. Unless large amounts of an acidic food (such as vinegar) are added, these low-acid foods must be processed in the higher heat of a pressure canner.

ACIDITY BOOSTERS Lemon juice and vinegar are highly acidic. They're often added to low-acid foods to control harmful bacteria that can't thrive in acidic environments.

That's why recipes for tomatoes, which have a fairly neutral pH, often call for adding lemon juice.

PROCESS IN BOILING-WATER CANNER

pH LEVEL	FOOD
2.0 to 2.9	Lemons, strawberries
3.0 to 3.9	Gooseberries, rhubarb, pickles, oranges, peaches, sauerkraut, apples, apricots, cherries, plums, blueberries, raspberries, blackberries, pears
4.0 to 4.6	Grapes, most tomato recipes

PROCESS IN PRESSURE CANNER

pH LEVEL	FOOD
4.7 to 4.9	Green beans, eggplant, some tomato recipes
5.0 to 5.9	Asparagus, carrots, pumpkin, sweet peppers, beets, turnips, sweet potatoes, onions, cauliflower, cabbage, okra
6.0 to 7.0	Peas, lima beans, corn, spinach

74

GEAR UP FOR CANNING

CANNING-SPECIFIC TOOLS

Here are some specialty tools that will make canning more efficient:

JAR LIFTER (A) This tool lifts jars firmly and securely in and out of hot water. Use two hands if possible and squeeze firmly.

MAGNETIC WAND (B) This magic wand enables you to drop lids and screw bands into hot water to sterilize and to soften the sealing compound on the lids and then easily lift the lids and bands from the hot water.

COMBINATION RULER/SPATULA (C) The tapered end of this somewhat flexible tool easily slips in along the sides of filled jars to release air bubbles. (It's important to get the bubbles out of a jar because if there is too much air in the jar, it can interfere with the process of forcing the extra air out of the top of the jar in order to get a good seal.) The calibrated, notched end matches the measurements of the most common required headspaces and is less awkward to use than a ruler to measure headspaces.

JAR FUNNEL (D) Wider and shorter than other funnels, jar funnels come in both wide-mouth and regular-mouth versions for use in wide-mouth and regular-mouth jars. They're invaluable for preventing spills when filling jars.

ORDINARY KITCHEN TOOLS

These basic kitchen tools are necessary for successful canning.

RULER (E) Use to measure headspace when filling jars or when a recipe specifies produce cut into certain lengths.

KITCHEN TOWELS (F) These have many uses when canning, besides drying wet utensils. Use to wipe rims of jars. Lay a dry towel on the counter to set hot jars on (never place hot jars directly on the counter; they may crack). And, of course, use them to wipe up spills.

TIMER (G) A timer is important to keep track of cooking and

processing times. The timer built into a stove works fine, but a portable timer easily slips into your pocket if you leave the room.

POT HOLDERS (H) One pair is essential, but two are better so you will always have a clean, dry pair (wet pot holders conduct heat, resulting in burns). Or try silicone pot holders–they clean up in a snap.

COLANDER (I) Use to wash and drain produce. Line with cheesecloth and set it over a bowl to strain juices for canned juice and jellies.

PERMANENT MARKER (J) Use to write on metal, paper, plastic, and glass. Once the ink is dry, it is fairly resistant to fading and moisture. Always label preserved foods with

contents and date so they can be eaten within the proper time frame.

MEASURING SPOONS (K) Most sets of measuring spoons have 1 tablespoon, 1 teaspoon, $\frac{1}{2}$ teaspoon, and $\frac{1}{4}$ teaspoon. Quality metal spoons cost just a bit more and like metal measuring cups, better release finely ground foods that might otherwise cling.

8-CUP (1.9-L) LIQUID MEASURE (L) Essential for measuring large amounts of chopped or sliced produce and for measuring large amounts of water and other liquids, it also makes a handy mixing bowl.

LADLES (M) Canning involves transferring liquids from one container to another, and a ladle

does that quickly and precisely. Metal is ideal because it won't melt if left too close to a burner. Sterilize ladles by dipping them in boiling water.

MEASURING CUPS (N) Use measuring cups for dry goods, such as sugar. (Use glass measures for liquids; they measure differently.) Durable metal cups let finely ground foods slide out more easily with no static cling. Most come in sets of 1 cup (250 ml), $\frac{1}{2}$ cup (125 ml), $\frac{1}{3}$ cup (75 ml), and $\frac{1}{4}$ cup (50 ml).

LARGE SIEVE (O) Use this like a small colander. Rinse off small amounts of berries or set over a bowl to strain bits from liquids. Or line with cheesecloth to finely strain small amounts of liquid.

75

PACK IT RAW OR HOT

Food is loaded into jars in one of two ways–the hot-pack or the raw-pack method. Here's how to determine which is better for your situation:

To achieve ideal flavor and texture, a recipe will follow either a hot-pack or raw-pack method.

Although the recipe might not refer to these names, it will instruct you to put food into a jar raw and top it with hot liquid or to cook the food first and pack it, still hot, into jars.

HOT PACK For food that is firm and processes well, this method is preferred. It's the better method for most fruits and vegetables, meats, poultry, and seafoods.

Simmer food in brine, water, juice, or syrup for a few minutes. Then load the food, still hot, into hot, sterilized jars.

Precooking the food this way breaks it down more to eliminate air so it's less likely to spoil and so food doesn't float. Also, more produce can be loaded into fewer jars and processing time is shorter because the food is already hot–a significant advantage if you're processing large amounts of food.

RAW PACK Also called cold pack, this method is better for foods that are more delicate and that would have a tough time standing up to a cooking process followed by the heat-intensive canning process.

Food is placed into the jar while still raw and packed in firmly but not crushed. Boiling brine, syrup, juice, or water is added if additional liquid is needed (the recipe will specify).

This method is fast and easy and helps preserve texture. However, it also may result in some shrinkage as food is processed, causing some foods to float to the top of the jar.

76

MEASURE HEADSPACE

Headspace is the distance betwen the surface of the food in the jar and the underside of the lid. The amount of headspace is specified by the recipe and is important to ensure that a jar develops a tight vacuum seal.

Too much headspace and your food will discolor and there may not be enough processing time to properly seal. Too little headspace and the food may bubble out and interfere with a proper seal.

Measure headspace with a ruler or canning tool from the top of the jar to the top of the liquid. It's okay if a little bit of solid food rises above the liquid; it will settle into the liquid over time.

77

STERILIZE JARS AND LIDS

Before filling, jars and lids need to be heated and sterilized in the canner or other hot water to ensure safely canned foods. The process isn't difficult, but follow these directions to do it correctly in record time:

STERILIZING JARS All jars must be cleaned and sterilized before using.

You can simply dip them in a large pan of simmering water for a few minutes and then load them, still hot, with food.

A more efficient way is to use the canner, which already has hot water in it. After filling the canner halfway and bringing the water to just below a simmer, put the jars in it, filling each jar with some hot water to prevent floating. If the canner has an adjustable rack, position it in the highest position. Cover with the lid to get the jars hot and steamy. They don't need to be submerged; the steam will sterilize them. After a few minutes, the jars are ready to fill.

Take out just one jar at a time, fill it, put on the lid, and return it to the canner to keep everything hot. Then take out another jar and fill it: one jar out, one jar in.

HEATING LIDS Before using lids, heat them to soften the sealing compound. Put the lids in the canner with the jars as you sterilize them. Or heat them in a saucepan by themselves if you wish.

Regardless, the water must be very hot (180°F [82°C]) to soften the compound but must not boil or the compound will start to break down.

Rings can also be sterilized, but it's not necessary. Instead you can wash them in hot, soapy water and rinse thoroughly.

ALL ABOUT LIDS

Lids are essentially flat disks of metal with a sticky compound around the edge. When heated, that compound softens, then cools, and creates a long-lasting seal.

Lids also have a raised circle in the center. After canning, if a vacuum seal has been created, that raised circle is sucked down and flattened. If the seal has not been properly created, you can press the circle with your finger and it will pop up and down. (In that case, refrigerate and eat the food within a few to several days.)

The function of bands is simply to hold the lids in place during processing and cooling. They can be reused many times unless they start to rust.

78 BOIL IT DOWN

The boiling-water method of canning is appropriate for high-acid foods, the most common of which is tomatoes. Here's how to put them up safely:

FILL THE JARS

The cold-pack method for tomatoes is shown here, but follow the exact process specified in your recipe.

STEP 1 Fill the jar. Pack the solids as tightly as you can without crushing; check headspace. Top with hot liquid as specified in the recipe, rechecking headspace.

STEP 2 Remove air bubbles. Insert a special canning tool or a thin, flexible spatula down along the sides of the jar to remove any air bubbles. Measure headspace again, adding or removing liquid as needed.

STEP 3 Wipe rim and threads of jar with a clean, damp cloth to remove any residue. Food particles or liquid left on the jar rim might interfere with the seal.

STEP 4 Set lid on jar and screw on band no more than fingertip tight, just tight enough that you could turn the band another ¼ to ½ inch (6–13 mm) tighter. If applied too tightly, the lids might not seal.

PROCESS THE JARS

Submerging the jars in boiling water heats and sterilizes the food inside and is the first step in creating a sealed jar.

STEP 5 Place jars in canner. As you fill each jar, set it back in the canner filled with simmering water. The canner shown has a rack with handles to hang on the canner rim so that jars sit halfway in the water.

STEP 6 Process jars. When all jars are filled, lower them into the canner. They should be covered with 1 to 2 inches (25–50 mm) water. Add more boiling water if needed to achieve this. Start processing time from the moment the water starts to boil. Keep at a low, rolling boil.

STEP 7 Remove jars. When processing time is up, turn off heat. Using pot holders, lift up the rack and rest handles on the side of the canner. Allow the jars to cool in place for a few minutes.

STEP 8 Cool. Remove jars from canner and set on a wire rack or a towel on the countertop (cold, bare countertops can crack jars). Do not tighten bands. Allow to cool 12 to 24 hours. After that time test the seal by firmly pressing your finger on the center of the lid. It should not give. If it makes a popping sound, it is not properly sealed.

79 CAN UNDER PRESSURE

Pressure-canning is appropriate for low-acid foods–the most common of which is green beans. Here's how to put them up safely:

FILL THE JARS

The hot-pack method for green beans is shown, but follow the exact process specified in your recipe. Before you start filling jars, pour 2 to 3 inches (50–75 mm) of water into the canner.

STEP 1 Fill one sterilized, clean jar at a time; do not fill a cooled jar. Pack the food in the jar as tightly as you can without crushing it. Use a funnel as needed to keep jar rims clean.

STEP 2 Top ingredients with the hot liquid as recipe directs. Measure headspace and adjust as needed.

STEP 3 Use a spatula to remove air bubbles. Add more water if needed to achieve the correct headspace. Wipe jar rim and threads with a clean cloth. Set lid in place and screw band on fingertip tight, just ¼ to ½ inch (6–13 mm) from very tight. This is important so air can escape for a proper seal.

STEP 4 Set the last jar in place. The water in the canner should come up only a few inches and not cover the jars. Only enough water to create steam is needed.

PROCESS THE JARS

Submerging the jars in boiling water heats and sterilizes the food inside and is the first step in creating a sealed jar.

STEP 5 Set the lid in place and twist so the handles lock it in place. Do not put on the pressure regulator yet.

STEP 6 Turn heat to high and allow a full head of steam to come out of the vent pipe. Allow to vent for 10 minutes. For a weighted-gauge canner, adjust weights on the pressure regulator, if needed, and set the pressure regulator on the vent pipe to plug it.

STEP 7 Start timing when pressure is reached. At end of processing time, remove canner from heat. Do not open the lid. Wait until the safety valve drops back down or the dial returns to zero. Remove the pressure regulator. Unlock the handles and open the canner away from you so that any steam is directed away from you.

STEP 8 Allow the jars to stand in the canner for 10 minutes to cool slightly. Remove them from the canner and set on a wire rack or a kitchen towel placed on the counter. Do not tighten lids. Let cool for 12 to 24 hours. Test seals by pressing on the lid (it should not pop up or down). Refrigerate any improperly sealed food to eat soon.

80

JAM ON IT!

Jam is made by cooking fruit with sugar until thick and the fruit is soft and spreadable.

Choose fruits at the peak of flavor and ripeness. Discard any fruit with even a hint of mildew–it might spoil the whole batch. Wash the fruit well and prepare as directed in the recipe–in most cases the fruit is mashed with a potato masher.

Combine fruit, sugar, pectin (if it's called for), and any flavorings in the pot. Use the size of pot specified in the recipe. The pot must be large enough so the pot will not overflow when the mixture boils.

Bring mixture to full rolling boil that cannot be stirred down (see Step 1). Some types of pectin are added after the mixture boils. Be sure to use the type of pectin called for in the recipe and to add it when specified in the method. Different types of pectin are added at different points in the jam-making process. As the mixture boils, foam will form on the surface of the mixture. Use a metal spoon to skim off the foam (see Step 2). Fill the jars as shown in Steps 3 to 5.

NO ADJUSTMENTS NEEDED

You may be tempted to tweak a recipe, but don't. Success in jam making depends on chemical reactions among ingredients in the correct proportions. Remember these tips:

MAKE THE AMOUNT OF JAM SPECIFIED IN THE RECIPE. Do not double the recipe or there may be problems with jelling or scorching in the pan.

USE THE AMOUNT OF SUGAR SPECIFIED; DON'T ALTER. Sugar interacts with pectin to create the ideal texture. It also acts as a preservative.

ACID IS NEEDED FOR JELLING AND FLAVOR. With low-acid fruits, the recipe will direct you to add bottled lemon juice or citric acid.

COOLING

Jams require time to set up. Allow the jars to cool on racks for 12 hours before moving them to long-term storage. Some recipes specify tilting or inverting the jars during cooling to distribute the pieces of fruit. Wait about 2 weeks before serving to give the jam time to set up.

STEP 1 Unless otherwise specified in the recipe, bring mixture to a full rolling boil. (The bubbles break the surface so rapidly you can't stir them down.)

STEP 2 Boiling makes foam. To skim off foam, gently glide a metal spoon over the surface and remove and discard the frothy bubbles.

STEP 3 For the cleanest, easiest way to fill jars with hot jam, use a canning funnel. A funnel helps prevent sticky jam from running down the outside of the jar.

STEP 4 When filling jars, leave the recommended headspace (the space between the top of the jam and the rim). Use a clean, damp cloth to wipe jar rims.

STEP 5 A magnetic wand makes transferring lids from hot water to the jars easy. Place hot lids on jars. Gently adjust screw bands over lids.

STEP 6 Cool the jars on wire racks at least 12 hours. Do not move the jars during cooling. Allow about 2 weeks before serving for the jam to set up completely. Some recipes call for inverting the jars for a brief period. Follow your recipe exactly.

81 SLATHER ON STRAWBERRY JAM

In the dead of winter, there is nothing like the flavor of jam made from summer-ripe strawberries.

PREP: 40 MINUTES   **PROCESS:** 5 MINUTES   **MAKES:** 9 HALF-PINTS (9 250-ML JARS)

- 12 cups (3 L) fresh strawberries
- 1 1.75-ounce (50-g) package regular powdered fruit pectin or 6 tablespoons classic powdered fruit pectin
- ½ teaspoon butter
- 7 cups (1.4 kg) sugar

STEP 1 In an 8-quart (8-L) heavy pot crush 1 cup (250 ml) of the strawberries with a potato masher. Continue adding berries and crushing, 1 cup (250 ml) at a time. Measure 5 cups (1.25 L) crushed berries; discard or save remaining crushed berries. Stir pectin and butter into the 5 cups (1.25 L) berries in pot.

STEP 2 Bring mixture to a full rolling boil, stirring constantly. Stir in sugar. Return to a full rolling boil, stirring constantly. Boil hard 1 minute, stirring constantly. Remove from heat. Quickly skim off foam with a metal spoon.

STEP 3 Ladle hot jam into hot, sterilized half-pint (125 ml) canning jars, leaving a ¼-inch (6-mm) headspace. Wipe jar rims; adjust lids and screw bands.

STEP 4 Process jars in a boiling-water canner 5 minutes (start timing when water returns to boiling). Cool on wire racks. Cool about 20 minutes, then gently turn and tilt jars to distribute fruit; repeat as needed. (Do not invert jars.)

PER 1 TABLESPOON: 39 cal., 0 g fat, 0 mg chol., 1 mg sodium, 10 g carb, 0 g fiber, 0 g pro.

82

ROCK SOME RASPBERRY JAM

When you have more raspberries than you can eat fresh, make this jewel-tone jam.

PREP: 35 MINUTES **PROCESS:** 5 MINUTES **MAKES:** 8 HALF-PINTS (8 125-ML JARS)

12	cups (3 L) fresh raspberries
1	1.75-oz. (50-g) package regular powdered fruit pectin or 6 tablespoons classic powdered fruit pectin
½	teaspoon butter
7	cups (1.4 kg) sugar

STEP 1 In an 8-quart (8-L) heavy pot crush 1 cup (250 ml) of the raspberries with a potato masher. Continue adding berries and crushing until you have 5 cups (1.25 L) crushed berries. Stir in pectin and butter.

STEP 2 Bring mixture to a full rolling boil, stirring constantly. Stir in sugar. Return to full rolling boil, stirring constantly. Boil hard 1 minute, stirring constantly. Remove from heat; quickly skim off foam with a metal spoon.

STEP 3 Ladle hot jam into hot, sterilized half-pint (250 ml) canning jars, leaving a ¼-inch (6-mm) headspace. Wipe jar rims; adjust lids and screw bands.

STEP 4 Process filled jars in a boiling-water canner 5 minutes (start timing when the water returns to boiling). Remove jars from canner; cool on wire rack.

TIP If you like, add one of the following to the fruit mixture along with the sugar: 1 teaspoon finely shredded lemon peel, ½ teaspoon ground nutmeg, or ¼ teaspoon grated fresh ginger.

PER 1 TABLESPOON: 46 cal., 0 g fat, 0 mg chol., 1 mg sodium, 12 g carb., 1 g fiber, 0 g pro.

83

BITE INTO THE BEST-EVER DILL PICKLES

Crunchy and redolent of dill, these are yummy straight from the jar or on a grilled burger.

PREP: 30 MINUTES **PROCESS:** 10 MINUTES **STAND:** 1 WEEK **MAKES:** 6 PINTS (6 250-ML JARS)

- **3** to 3¼ pounds (1.25–1.50 kg) 4-inch (10 cm) pickling cucumbers (about 36 small)
- **4** cups (1 L) water
- **4** cups (1 L) white vinegar
- **½** cup (100 g) sugar
- **⅓** cup (100 g) pickling salt
- **6** tablespoons dill seeds

STEP 1 Thoroughly scrub cucumbers in cold running water. (Be sure they are unwaxed.) Remove stems and blossoms; slice off blossom ends. Slice cucumbers into ¼- to ½-inch-thick slices (6–13 mm).

STEP 2 In a 4- to 5-qt. (4–5 L) stainless-steel, enamel, or nonstick heavy pot combine the water, vinegar, sugar, and pickling salt. Bring mixture to boiling, stirring until sugar dissolves.

STEP 3 Pack cucumber slices loosely into hot, sterilized pint jars, leaving a ½-inch (13-mm) headspace. Add 1 tablespoon dill seeds to each jar. Pour hot vinegar mixture over cucumbers, maintaining ½-inch (13-mm) headspace. Discard remaining vinegar mixture. Wipe jar rims; adjust lids.

STEP 4 Process filled jars in a boiling-water canner 10 minutes (start timing when water returns to boiling). Remove jars from canner; cool on wire racks. Allow to stand at room temperature 1 week before serving.

PER ¼ CUP (35 G): 25 cal., 0 g fat, 0 mg chol., 859 mg sodium, 5 g carbo., 0 g fiber, 0 g pro.

CRUNCHY DILL AND ONION CHIPS In a large bowl combine 12 cups (3 L) sliced pickling cucumbers, 2 cups (300 g) thinly sliced onions, and ⅓ cup (100 g) pickling salt. Set a large stainless-steel or nonmetal colander in an extra-large stainless-steel or nonmetal bowl; in colander alternately layer cucumber mixture and crushed ice, ending with a layer of ice. Weight down mixture with a heavy plate. Chill in the refrigerator overnight or up to 24 hours. Remove any unmelted ice from cucumber mixture; discard any liquid in bowl. In a 4- to 5-quart (4–5 L) stainless-steel, enamel, or nonstick heavy pot combine 4 cups (1 L) water, 4 cups (1 L) white vinegar, and ½ cup (100 g) sugar. Bring mixture to boiling, stirring until sugar dissolves. Pack cucumbers and onions in jars as directed in Step 3 and continue as directed through Step 4. Makes 5 pints (250 ml).

84 GET SWEET ON PICKLES

Turmeric gives these bread and butter pickles a touch of sunny yellow color.

PREP: 40 MINUTES **CHILL:** 3 TO 12 HOURS **PROCESS:** 10 MINUTES **MAKES:** 7 PINTS (7 250-ML JARS)

16	cups (3.75 L) sliced small to medium pickling cucumbers*
8	medium white onions, sliced
⅓	cup (100 g) pickling salt
3	cloves garlic, halved
	Crushed ice
4	cups (800 g) sugar
3	cups (750 ml) cider vinegar
2	tablespoons mustard seeds
1½	teaspoons celery seeds
1½	teaspoons ground turmeric

STEP 1 In a 6- to 8-quart (6–8 L) stainless-steel, enamel, or nonstick pot combine cucumbers, onions, pickling salt, and garlic. Add 2 inches (5 cm) of crushed ice. Cover and chill 3 to 12 hours.

STEP 2 Remove any unmelted ice from pot. Transfer cucumber mixture to a large colander and drain. Remove and discard garlic pieces.

STEP 3 In the same pot combine sugar, vinegar, mustard seeds, celery seeds, and turmeric. Bring mixture to boiling, stirring to dissolve sugar. Stir in cucumber mixture. Return to boiling; remove from heat.

STEP 4 Pack hot cucumber mixture and liquid into hot sterilized pint (250 ml) canning jars, leaving a ½-inch (13 mm) headspace. Wipe jar rims; adjust lids and screw bands.

STEP 5 Process filled jars in a boiling-water canner 10 minutes (start timing when water returns to boiling). Remove jars from canner; cool on wire racks.

*TIP Before using pickling cucumbers (often called Kirby cucumbers), thoroughly scrub them with a soft vegetable brush in plenty of cold running water. Remove the stems and blossoms; slice off blossom ends. Use a mandoline to create perfectly even cucumber slices. If pickling cucumbers are not available, use regular cucumbers from your garden or farmers market–just be sure they have not been coated in wax, which interferes with the pickling process.

PER ¼ CUP (35 G): 33 cal., 0 g fat, 0 mg chol., 200 mg sodium, 9 g carb., 0 g fiber, 0 g pro.

85 PICKLE DILLY GREEN BEANS

These spicy, dilly beans make a delicious accompaniment to hearty grilled steak or roast beef.

PREP: 45 MINUTES **COOK:** 5 MINUTES **PROCESS:** 5 MINUTES **MAKES:** 5 PINTS (5 250-ML JARS)

- 3 pounds (1.4 kg) fresh green beans
- 5 fresh Thai or red serrano chile peppers* (optional)
- 3 cups (750 ml) water
- 3 cups (750 ml) white wine vinegar
- 3 tablespoons snipped fresh dill or 1 tablespoon dried dill
- 1 tablespoon pickling salt
- 1 tablespoon sugar
- 6 cloves garlic, minced
- ½ teaspoon crushed red pepper or 1 Thai chile pepper, finely chopped*
- 5 small heads fresh dill (optional)

STEP 1 Wash beans; drain. If desired, remove ends and strings. Leave beans whole. In an uncovered 8-quart (8 L) pot cook beans and the 5 fresh chile peppers (if using) in enough boiling water to cover 5 minutes; drain.

STEP 2 Pack hot beans lengthwise into hot, sterilized pint canning jars, cutting beans to fit if necessary and leaving a ¹/₂-inch (13 mm) headspace. Add 1 of the boiled chile peppers (if using) to each jar. Set aside.

STEP 3 In a large stainless-steel, enamel, or nonstick heavy saucepan combine the water, vinegar, snipped or dried dill, pickling salt, sugar, garlic, and crushed red pepper. Bring to boiling, stirring until sugar dissolves.

STEP 4 Pour hot liquid over beans in jars, leaving a ¹/₂-inch (13 mm) headspace. If desired, add a head of fresh dill to each jar. Wipe jar rims; adjust lids.

STEP 5 Process jars in a boiling-water canner 5 minutes (start timing when water returns to boiling); cool on wire racks.

PER ½ CUP (75 G): 42 cal., 0 g fat, 0 mg chol., 357 mg sodium, 7 g carb., 3 g fiber, 2 g pro.

*TIP Chile peppers contain oils that can burn your skin and eyes. If your bare hands come in contact with a cut piece of chile, wash hands well with soap and warm water.

86 CAN YOUR OWN TOMATOES

Tomatoes are probably the most popular produce for canning—and perfect for beginners.

PREP: 15 MINUTES   **PROCESS:** 1 HOUR 25 MINUTES   **MAKES:** 8 PINTS (8 250-ML JARS) OR 4 QUARTS (4 L JARS)

1¼ to 1½ pounds (570–680 g) ripe tomatoes for pint jars (250 ml) or 2½ to 3½ pounds (1.1–1.3 kg) for quart (1 L) jars

Bottled lemon juice

STEP 1 Bring a large pot of water to boiling. Cut a shallow X in blossom ends. Working in batches, lower tomatoes into boiling water 30 to 60 seconds or until skins start to split. Use a slotted spoon to transfer tomatoes to large bowl of ice water. Peel skins off tomatoes. If desired, cut tomatoes in half.

STEP 2 Pack tomatoes into hot, sterilized pint or quart canning jars, pressing the tomatoes until spaces between tomatoes are filled with juice. Leave a ½-inch (6-mm) headspace. Add 1 tablespoon lemon juice to each pint or 2 tablespoons lemon juice to each quart. If desired, add ¼ to ½ teaspoon salt to each pint or ½ to 1 teaspoon salt to each quart. Wipe jar rims; adjust lids and screw bands.

STEP 3 Process filled pint or quart jars in a boiling-water canner 85 minutes (start timing when water returns to boiling). Remove jars; cool on wire racks.

HOT-PACK TOMATOES IN WATER
Prepare tomatoes as directed and place in pot; add enough water to cover. Bring to boiling; reduce heat. Simmer, uncovered, 5 minutes. Pack jars with tomatoes and cooking liquid, leaving a ½-inch (13 mm) headspace. Add lemon juice and, if desired, salt. Wipe jar rims; adjust lids and screw bands. Process in a boiling-water canner 40 minutes for pints (250 ml), 45 minutes for quarts (1 L); start timing when water returns to boiling. Remove jars; cool on wire racks.

RAW-PACK TOMATOES IN WATER
Prepare tomatoes and fill jars as directed. Pour boiling water into each jar, maintaining the ½-inch (13 mm) headspace. Wipe jar rims; adjust lids and screw bands. Process in a boiling-water canner 40 minutes for pints (250 ml), 45 minutes for quarts (1 L) (start timing when water returns to boiling). Remove jars; cool on wire racks.

PER ¼ CUP (60 ML): 13 cal., 0 g fat, 0 mg chol., 4 mg sodium, 3 g carb., 1 g fiber, 1 g pro.

87

GET SAUCY

Vary the amount of sugar you add to this applesauce to make it as tart or as sweet as you like.

PREP: 1 HOUR   **COOK:** 25 MINUTES   **PROCESS:** 15 MINUTES   **MAKES:** 6 PINTS (6 250-ML JARS) OR 3 QUARTS (3 L JARS)

- **8** pounds (3.6 kg) tart cooking apples (about 24 medium)
- **2** cups (500 ml) water
- **10** inches (25 cm) stick cinnamon(optional)
- **¾** to 1¼ cups (150–250 g) sugar

STEP 1 Core and quarter apples. In an 8- to 10-quart (8–10 L) heavy pot combine apples, the water, and, if desired, cinnamon. Bring to boiling; reduce heat. Simmer, covered, 25 to 35 minutes or until apples are very tender, stirring often.

STEP 2 Remove and discard cinnamon if used. Press apples through a food mill or sieve. Return pulp to pot. Stir in enough of the sugar to sweeten as desired. If necessary, stir in an additional ½ to 1 cup (125–250 ml) water to make desired consistency. Bring to boiling, stirring constantly.

STEP 3 Ladle hot applesauce into hot, sterilized pint (250 ml) or quart (1 L) canning jars, leaving a ½-inch (13 mm) headspace. Wipe jar rims; adjust lids and screw bands.

STEP 4 Process filled jars in a boiling-water canner 15 minutes for pints (250 ml) or 20 minutes for quarts (1 L) (start timing when water returns to boiling). Remove jars from canner; cool on wire racks.

PER ½ CUP (125 ML): 80 cal., 0 g fat, 0 mg chol., 1 mg sodium, 21 g carb., 2 g fiber, 0 g pro.

CALVADOS-CRANBERRY APPLESAUCE Prepare as directed, except stir in 1 cup (250 ml) Calvados (or other apple brandy) and 1 cup (150 g) dried cranberries or golden raisins with the sugar.

GINGER-HONEY APPLESAUCE Prepare as directed, except substitute honey for the sugar. Stir in 1 cup (150 g) finely chopped crystallized ginger before ladling into jars.

MAPLE APPLESAUCE Prepare as directed, except substitute pure maple syrup for the sugar.

88

FREEZE YOUR ASSETS

Freezing is the quickest and easiest way to preserve fresh produce. These tips (and the charts in #90) provide all the information you need to fill your freezer.

EQUIPMENT

PANS AND UTENSILS You need a colander and a large pot or saucepan that has a wire basket. An accurate freezer thermometer will help you regulate your freezer temperature to 0°F (-18°C) or below.

FREEZER CONTAINERS

Use containers and packing materials that are durable, easy to seal, resistant to cracking at low temperatures, and moisture- and vapor-resistant. Choose the right size container for your volume; wasted space can lead to oxidation and freezer burn. Foods containing water expand when frozen, so make sure containers are expandable or leave enough headspace to allow for expansion. The following options are suitable for frozen foods.

RIGID CONTAINERS Use sealable, rigid glass or plastic containers designed for freezing.

CANNING JARS Select canning jars approved for freezing–this information is clearly noted on the packaging. Use only wide-mouth glass jars. To allow for expansion, do not fill jars above the 1-inch line.

PLASTIC FREEZER BAGS Use bags designated for freezing, such as resealable bags and vacuum freezer bags. These are made of thicker plastic than regular bags and are more resistant to moisture and oxygen. In lieu of a vacuum sealer, use a straw to suck air out of bags.

GENERAL FREEZING STEPS

STEP 1 Select fruits and vegetables at peak maturity. Rinse and drain small quantities through several changes of cold water. Lift fruits and vegetables out of the water; do not let them soak. Prepare cleaned produce for freezing as specified in #90.

STEP 2 Blanch vegetables (and fruits when directed) by scalding in boiling water for the specified time. This stops or slows enzymes that can cause loss of flavor and color and toughen the food. Timings vary with vegetable type and size.

Blanching is a heat-and-cool process. Fill a large pot with water, using 1 gallon (3.75 L) of water per 1 pound (.5 kg) of prepared food. Bring to boiling. Add prepared food to the boiling water (or place in a wire basket and lower into the water); cover. Start timing immediately. Cook over high heat for the time specified in the charts. (Add 1 minute if you live 5,000 feet [1,524 meters] or higher above sea level.) Near the end of the time, fill your sink or a large container with ice water. When boiling time is complete, use a slotted spoon to remove the food from the boiling water or lift the wire basket out of the water. Immediately plunge food into ice water. Chill for the same amount of time it was boiled; drain.

STEP 3 Spoon food into containers or bags, leaving specified headspace. Fruits are often frozen with sugar or liquid for better texture and flavor. Refer to the chart in #90. Pack as directed. These are the packing methods referred to in the chart:

UNSWEETENED OR DRY PACK Do not add sugar or liquid to fruit; pack in a container. This is best for small whole fruits, such as berries.

WATER PACK Cover the fruit with water or unsweetened fruit juice. Do not use glass jars. Maintain the recommended headspace.

SUGAR PACK Place a small amount of fruit in the container and sprinkle lightly with sugar; repeat layering. Cover and let stand about 15 minutes or until juicy; seal.

SYRUP PACK Cover fruit with a syrup of sugar and water. For a very thin syrup, use 1 cup sugar (200 g) and 4 cups (1 L) water to yield about 4 cups (1 L) syrup. For a thin syrup, use $1^2/_3$ cups (330 g) sugar and 4 cups water (1 L) to yield about $4^1/_4$ cups (1 L) syrup. For a medium syrup, use $2^2/_3$ cups (530 g) sugar and 4 cups (1 L) water to yield about $4^2/_3$ cups (1.1 L) syrup. For a heavy syrup, use 4 cups (800 g) sugar and 4 cups (1 L) water to yield about $5^3/_4$ cups (1.4 L) syrup.

STEP 4 If using containers, wipe rims. Seal bags or containers according to manufacturer's directions, pressing out as much air as possible. If necessary, use freezer tape around lid edges for a tight seal.

STEP 5 Label each container or bag with its contents, amount, and date. Lay bags flat; add packages to the freezer in batches to make sure food freezes quickly. Leave space between packages so air can circulate around them. When frozen solid, the packages can be placed closer together.

USING FROZEN FOODS

Vegetables are best cooked from a frozen state. Thaw fruits in their containers either in the refrigerator or in a bowl of cold water. Use frozen fruits and vegetables within 8 to 10 months.

89 CREATE YOUR OWN HERBED VEGETABLE BLEND

Choose a flavored butter to freeze with this rainbow of fresh veggies.

PREP: 45 MINUTES   **FREEZE:** 2 HOURS   **MAKES:** FOUR 3-SERVING PORTIONS

½   cup butter, softened (125 g)

   Desired Seasoning Mix

¼   teaspoon salt

2   ears of corn, husks and silks removed

2   cups broccoli and/or cauliflower florets (350 g)

3   medium carrots, bias-sliced ¼ inch thick (6 mm)

1½   cups yellow summer squash and/ or zucchini bias-sliced ½ inch thick (250 g, sliced 1 cm thick)

1   large red or yellow sweet pepper, seeded and cut into bite-size strips

1   small sweet onion, cut into thin wedges

STEP 1 For herb butter, in a bowl combine butter, Seasoning Mix, and salt. Shape into a 5-inch (13 cm) roll. Wrap in plastic wrap. Freeze about 1 hour or until firm. Cut into eight slices. Place in freezer container; freeze until needed.

STEP 2 In a covered 6-quart (6 L) pot cook corn in enough boiling water to cover 1 minute. Add broccoli, carrots, and squash. Cook, covered, 2 minutes; drain. Plunge vegetables into a large bowl of ice water. Let stand until chilled. Cut kernels from cobs. Using a slotted spoon, transfer remaining vegetables to a paper towel-lined tray; pat dry.

STEP 3 Line a 15×10×1-inch (40×25×2-cm) baking pan with parchment paper or foil. In the prepared pan spread corn, drained vegetables, sweet pepper, and onion in an even layer. Freeze about 1 hour or until nearly firm.

STEP 4 Spoon 1½ cups (150 g) vegetables into each quart (1 L) freezer bag. Add 2 slices butter to each bag. Squeeze air from bag. Seal and label. Freeze up to 6 months.

HEATING DIRECTIONS Place one portion of frozen vegetables in a saucepan. Cook, covered, over medium heat 5 to 10 minutes or until vegetables are heated through, stirring occasionally. Season with salt and black pepper.

PER ½ CUP (50 G): 106 cal., 8 g fat (5 g sat. fat), 20 mg chol., 136 mg sodium, 8 g carb., 2 g fiber, 2 g pro.

ASIAN SEASONING MIX Combine 1 tablespoon. grated fresh ginger, 2 cloves minced garlic, and 3 drops toasted sesame oil.

SOUTHWESTERN SEASONING MIX Combine 1 teaspoon ground ancho chile pepper; ½ teaspoon dried oregano, crushed; and ½ teaspoon finely shredded lime peel.

ITALIAN SEASONING MIX Combine 2 cloves minced garlic and ½ teaspoon dried Italian seasoning, crushed.

90

GO COLD

Follow these freezing methods and you'll have a
freezer full of produce that tastes almost garden fresh.

FREEZE FRUITS

Read "Freeze Your Assets" (#88). Wash fresh fruits with cool, clear tap water but do not soak them; drain.
Follow preparation directions, below. If you choose to freeze fruits with syrup, select the syrup that best suits
the fruit and your taste (see #88). Allow ½ to ⅔ cup (125–150 ml) syrup for each 2 cups (500 ml) fruit.

FOOD	PREPARATION	FREEZING
Apples, Pears	Allow 2 to 3 pounds (1–1.4 kg) per quart (1 L). For apples, select varieties that are crisp, not mealy, in texture. Peel and core; halve, quarter, or slice. Dip into ascorbic acid color keeper solution; drain.	Use a syrup, sugar, or unsweetened pack, leaving the recommended headspace.*
Apricots, Nectarines, Peaches	Allow 2 to 3 pounds (1–1.4 kg) per quart (1 L). To peel peaches (peeling nectarines and apricots is not necessary), immerse in boiling water 30 to 60 seconds or until skins start to split; remove and plunge into cold water. Halve and pit. If desired, slice. Treat with ascorbic acid color keeper solution; drain.	Use a syrup, sugar, or water pack, leaving the recommended headspace.*
Berries	Allow 1 to 3 pounds (.5–1.4 kg) per quart (1 L). Can or freeze blackberries, blueberries, currants, elderberries, gooseberries, huckleberries, loganberries, and mulberries. Freeze (do not can) boysenberries, raspberries, and strawberries.	Slice strawberries if desired. Freeze boysenberries and raspberries whole. Use a syrup, sugar, or unsweetened pack, leaving the recommended headspace.*
Cherries	Allow 2 to 3 pounds (1–1.4 kg) per quart (1 L). If desired, treat with ascorbic acid color keeper solution; drain. If unpitted, prick skin on opposite sides to prevent splitting.	Use a syrup, sugar, or unsweetened pack, leaving the recommended headspace.*
Melons	Allow about 4 pounds (2 kg) per quart (1 L) for cantaloupe, honeydew, and watermelon. Peel and cut into ½-inch (13 mm) cubes or balls.	Use a syrup or unsweetened pack, leaving the recommended headspace.*
Plums	Allow 1 to 2 pounds (.5–1 kg) per quart (1 L). Prick skin on two sides. Freestone varieties may be halved and pitted.	Halve and pit. Treat with ascorbic acid color keeper solution; drain well. Use a syrup pack, leaving the recommended headspace.*
Rhubarb	Allow 1½ pounds (680 g) per quart (1 L). Discard leaves and woody ends. Cut into ½- to 1-inch pieces (1–2.5 cm). Freeze for best quality.	Blanch 1 minute; cool quickly and drain. Use a syrup or unsweetened pack or use a sugar pack of ½ cup sugar (100 g) to each 3 cups (700 ml) fruit, leaving the recommended headspace.*

*When freezing an unsweetened (dry) pack, leave a ½-inch (13 mm) headspace unless otherwise directed. When freezing a sugar, sugar syrup,
or water pack, leave a ½-inch (13-mm) headspace for pints (250 ml) and a 1-inch (2.5-cm) headspace for quarts (1 L).

FREEZE VEGETABLES

Wash fresh vegetables with cool, clear tap water; scrub firm vegetables with a clean produce brush to remove any dirt.

VEGETABLE	PREPARATION	FREEZING
Asparagus	Allow 2½ to 4½ pounds (1–2 kg) per quart (1 L). Wash; scrape off scales. Break off woody bases where spears snap easily; wash again. Sort by thickness. Leave whole or cut into 1-inch (2.5 cm) lengths.	Blanch small spears 2 minutes, medium 3 minutes, and large 4 minutes. Cool quickly by plunging into ice water; drain. Fill containers; shake down, leaving no headspace.
Beans: green, Italian, snap, or wax	Allow 1½ to 2½ pounds (.5–1 kg) per quart (1 L). Wash; remove ends and strings. Leave whole or cut into 1-inch (2.5 cm) pieces.	Blanch 3 minutes. Cool quickly by plunging into ice water; drain. Fill containers; shake down, leaving a ½-inch (13 mm) headspace.*
Beets	Allow 3 pounds (without tops) (1.4 kg) per quart (1 L). Trim off beet tops, leaving 1 inch (2.5 cm) of stem and roots, to reduce bleeding of color. Scrub well.	Cook unpeeled beets in boiling water until tender. (Allow 25 to 30 minutes for small beets; 45 to 50 minutes for medium beets.) Cool quickly by plunging into ice water; drain. Peel; remove stem and roots. Cut into slices or cubes. Fill containers, leaving a ½-inch (13 mm) headspace.*
Carrots	Use 1- to 1¼-inch-diameter (2–3-cm) carrots (larger carrots might be too fibrous). Allow 2 to 3 pounds (1 to 1.4 kg) per quart (1 L). Wash, trim, peel, and rinse again. Leave tiny ones whole; slice or dice the remainder.	Blanch tiny whole carrots 5 minutes and cut-up carrots 2 minutes. Cool quickly by plunging into ice water; drain. Pack tightly into containers, leaving a ½-inch (13 mm) headspace.*
Corn, whole kernel	Allow 4 to 5 pounds (1.8–2.3 kg) per quart (1 L). Remove husks. Scrub with a vegetable brush to remove silks. Wash and drain.	Cover ears with boiling water; return to boiling and boil 4 minutes. Cool by plunging into ice water; drain. Cut corn from cobs at two-thirds depth of kernels; do not scrape. Fill containers, leaving a ½-inch (13 mm) headspace.*
Peas: English or green	Allow 2 to 2½ pounds (1–1.25 kg) per pint (250 ml). Wash, shell, rinse, and drain.	Blanch 1½ minutes. Cool quickly by plunging into ice water; drain. Fill containers; shake down, leaving a ½-inch (13 mm) headspace.*
Peppers, chile	Select firm jalapeño or other chile peppers; wash. Halve large peppers. Remove stems, seeds, and membranes. Place, cut sides down, on a foil-lined baking sheet. Roast in a 425°F (220°C) oven 20 to 25 minutes or until skins are bubbly and brown. Cover peppers or wrap in foil and let stand about 15 minutes or until cool. Pull skins off gently and slowly, using a paring knife.	Package in freezer containers, leaving no headspace.
Peppers, sweet	Select firm green, bright red, orange, or yellow peppers; wash. Remove stems, seeds, and membranes. Place, cut sides down, on a foil-lined baking sheet. Roast in a 425°F (220°C) oven 20 to 25 minutes or until skins are bubbly and brown. Cover peppers or wrap in foil and let stand about 15 minutes or until cool. Pull the skins off gently and slowly, using a paring knife.	Quarter large pepper pieces or cut into strips. Fill containers, leaving a ½-inch (13 mm) headspace.* Or spread peppers in a single layer on a baking sheet; freeze until firm. Fill containers; shake to pack closely, leaving no headspace.

CHAPTER 5

Small Livestock

Nothing says "homestead" quicker than a colorful flock of chickens wandering through the yard. Oh, and a crowing rooster! Add to that beautiful scene some quacking ducks, fuzzy rabbits, grazing sheep, and curious goats, and you'll have a menagerie that is as fun as it is functional.

91

GET A FEATHERED BFF

Hens can become attentive, friendly pets. When you handle chicks, they become tame over time and will grow up to be friendly birds. Plus, these pets lay eggs! Some laying breeds will produce an egg a day nearly all of the year.

92

MEET THE CHICKEN

Here are some fun facts about chickens.

1 You don't need a rooster in order for hens to lay eggs. You only need a rooster if you want chicks.

2 One hen generally lays one egg a day, producing up to 300 eggs a year.

3 The average life span of a hen is 8 to 10 years; some hens live to age 20.

4 Hens start laying eggs at about 6 months old.

5 Chickens have a range of personality types, from friendly and curious to aloof and bossy.

6 Chickens "talk" and have numerous vocalizations that mean different things.

7 Chickens have good memories and can recognize facial features.

8 Chickens with red earlobes lay brown eggs; chickens with white earlobes lay white eggs.

9 As hens mature, they lay fewer but larger eggs.

10 Chickens drop their feathers and grow new ones each fall.

93 RAISE BEAUTIFUL EGG LAYERS

These breeds stand out amid the hundreds of chicken breeds available. All make excellent additions to any backyard poultry flock.

AMERAUCANA Loved for their blue eggs, these medium-size chickens come in a range of colors, such as buff, black, blue, blue-wheaten, brown-red, silver, wheaten, and white.

BUFF COCHIN These big exotic birds are covered in layers of golden feathers. Among the showiest backyard chickens, they make wonderful pets.

WHITE LEGHORN These hens lay big white eggs—lots of them. If you want a consistent source of high-quality large eggs, White Leghorns should be part of your flock.

SILVER LACED WYANDOTTE With silvery white and green iridescent feathers covering shapely, roundish bodies, this is a popular breed for showing in competitions.

BLACK AUSTRALORP This handsome hen hails from Australia and sports lovely black shiny feathers that, in sunlight, show hints of purple and green iridescence.

WHITE CRESTED BLACK POLISH The white-and-black feathered top knot on this breed adds elegance and comedy to the barnyard. This feature also makes it great for shows.

BLACK COPPER MARAN This attractive black French breed lays chocolate brown eggs—the darkest eggs in the brown egg spectrum.

BUFF ORPINGTON Originally from England, these large, shapely birds feature luminous golden feathers and striking red combs. These chickens are real beauties.

RHODE ISLAND RED This heavy mahogany red hen sports a jaunty red comb and is a favorite for backyard flocks because it is an egg-producing machine. Rhodies are also very hardy.

LIGHT BRAHMA Among the largest hens, Light Brahmas descended from Asian chickens and were brought to America in 1850. They have small combs (called pea combs) and two-tone feathers.

DELAWARE Developed in Delaware, this 1940s-era breed is a cross of Barred Rock roosters and New Hampshire hens. The breed features a predominantly white body with black barred accents.

WELSUMMER The brown and black speckled feathers on Welsummer hens resemble those of partridges. Bred in the Netherlands, this breed lays attractive brown speckled eggs.

94

KNOW HOMESTEAD CHICKEN BASICS

Easy to care for and friendly, chickens require secure living quarters and daily feed and water. But there are a few things to consider before you buy your first fuzzy chicks.

START SMALL A great starter flock consists of three to six female birds. A flock this size will easily produce more than a dozen eggs a week. Keep in mind that small chicks become large birds that require more space, larger quantities of feed, and more time to tidy the coop. Start with a small flock and add birds after you have a chance to experience how chickens fit into your lifestyle.

CONSIDER CLIMATE Raising chickens in northern climates, where temperatures regularly drop below freezing, requires a couple of simple provisions. Access to electricity is helpful to maintain open drinking water from a heated waterer during winter months. Also, a fully enclosed, draft-free coop protects birds in extreme cold and promotes egg production in the heart of winter.

KEEP CLEAN Use straw or wood shavings as bedding material in chicken coops. Change out bedding every couple of weeks or more frequently depending on how many birds you own.

FEED AND WATER Purchase mixed feed from a farm store. Manufactured chicken feeds include mixed poultry corn, chick crumbs, growers' pellets, layers' mash, and layers' pellets; choose the food that matches your chicken flock. A 6-week-old chick requires approximately 2 ounces (57 g) per day, divided between chick crumbs and corn. A grower of 12 weeks needs 3 ounces (85 g) per day, divided between growers' or layers' pellets or mash and corn. A laying hen will eat 4½ ounces (128 g) per day, divided between pellets or mash and corn. In addition to purchased feed, chickens can also eat table scraps and weeds from the garden. In fact, lettuce, cabbage, and other greens help make egg yolks more orange. Chickens also enjoy bread crusts, cake, and stale cookies, but avoid salty foods, banana skins, orange peels, and tea bags. Water towers for chickens are best, but a small bucket will also work as long as they can reach the water.

ADD SUPPLEMENTS Ground oyster shells provide calcium needed to make strong eggshells. Chickens also need grit, which they use in their gizzards to grind up food.

95

BRING HOME BABY CHICKS

Whether you hatch fertilized eggs in an incubator or order baby chicks through the mail, getting started with a new group of chicks is very exciting. If arriving in the mail, make sure the chicks have a healthy appearance. If you're hatching chicks, move them to a warm location as soon as they hatch.

SET UP A BROODER This is a place for the chicks to live, grow, eat, and drink for the first 3 to 5 weeks of their lives. Use a sturdy cardboard box, like those used by moving companies. Spread a layer of fresh wood shavings or straw.

ADD HEAT Use an artificial heat source, such as a heat lamp, to keep chicks warm; this replaces the warmth they would normally get from a mother hen.

FEED THE RIGHT FOOD A good quality starter feed, which can be purchased at your local feed store, is best for new chicks. Don't buy less expensive scratch feed, which can be difficult for young chicks to digest because the particles are too big. Starter feed has the vitamins and minerals chicks need.

PROVIDE WATER Use a shallow container so chicks can drink easily.

They will step into the water with their dirty feet, so change it twice a day.

MOVE CHICKS Chicks can be moved into a regular chicken coop at 3 to 5 weeks of age. Once in the coop, chicks should be sectioned off from older birds. They can also start eating a grower feed at this point.

96

PRACTICE CHICK SAFETY

You'll be smitten by your first chicks with their fluffy bodies and black shiny eyes. Here are some safety considerations for you and them:

WASH UP Make sure to wash hands before and after handling the birds to prevent the spread of bacteria that birds carry.

TAME DOWN Holding chicks is the best way to help tame them and show that you are a friend, not a foe.

MONITOR KIDS With supervision, children can hold chicks. Make sure that small children are very gentle as chicks are fragile.

WATCH PETS Keep an eye on any family pets nearby, such as cats and dogs, who may find the darting movement and cheeping sounds of chicks irresistible.

97

BUILD A BETTER CHICKEN COOP

When raising chickens, one of the most important decisions to make is how the chickens will be housed. Most chicken breeds are hardy, but care must be taken if you want happy and healthy chickens.

CONSIDER SIZE Layer chickens need 1½ to 2 square feet (140–90 square cm) of coop space. Meat birds and bantam breeds require slightly more and less, respectively. Various health issues, including egg-eating and cannibalism, have been linked to space issues. Save yourself time in the future by making sure your flock has enough room to spread their wings and move around.

PROVIDE FRESH AIR A chicken coop without proper ventilation may experience a buildup of toxic fumes, to say nothing about the smell. Your chickens will enjoy some fresh air with windows that open and a screened door.

KEEP IT WARM (AND COOL) Insulation is especially important in climates that experience very cold winters and very hot summers. Properly insulating your chicken coop will not only help keep your chickens comfortable, but it will also cut down on heating costs when the temperatures drop. Another way of heating a chicken house is to use solar. By placing clear panels on your coop during the winter, light still filters in and

warms up the coop while offering a measure of protection from the elements.

PROVIDE ROOSTING AND NESTING SPACE All chickens like to sleep off of the ground. Make sure your roosts are the right circumference so that your chickens can comfortably perch on them, and place the roosts at a height of approximately 1½ feet (46 cm) off of the ground. Also, provide nesting boxes so hens have a quiet place to lay eggs. This will make collecting eggs much easier.

ADD A CHICKEN RUN A run is a wire enclosure that allows chickens to leave the coop while still being contained and protected from predators outside. You may need to install a simple lean-to to give your chickens some shade during the warmer season.

LET THERE BE LIGHT As the days get shorter and cooler, many hens stop or slow down egg production. It takes about 12 hours of daylight to stimulate the birds to lay eggs. Setting a timer on a lightbulb might convince them to keep laying. The type of lighting used doesn't matter, and it doesn't take much. One incandescent lightbulb will keep 15 to 20 chickens happy so they can see, walk around and eat, and be stimulated by the light.

DISCOURAGE PESTS Rats and mice won't only eat into your feed costs, they can also carry diseases. Consider using flooring material in your coop that is rodent-resistant (e.g., concrete) and make sure your walls and fencing are secure. Rodents are particularly attracted to places where food is stored. If you can't find their entry points, store foods and grains in rodentproof containers.

98

COLLECT COLORFUL EGGS

If you want a rainbow of eggs (blues, greens, roses, olive, khaki), consider crossbred chickens. The chickens won't qualify for 4-H or county/state fair competitions because they are not purebred, but they will still supply you with plenty of colorful eggs.

EASTER EGGERS These crossbred hens with Ameraucana genetics produce an array of striking blue, green, rose, and cream eggs.

CREAM LEGBARS A cross of Barred Rock, Golden Leghorn, and Araucana chickens, these hens lay blue eggs.

OLIVE EGGERS This chicken is a crossbreed of a blue egg layer (such as a Cream Legbar or Ameraucana) and a brown egg layer (such as a Maran). Its eggs are olive green.

99

QUACK UP ON YOUR ACREAGE

EGGS, MEAT, OR SHOW? Whether you are looking to supplement your food supply with eggs and fresh meat or are interested in showing them at a fair, raising domestic ducks is a great idea. And there are so many choices. Bantam and ornamental ducks are fun for hobbyists and those who might want to show their ducks at an exhibition. A few Bantam breeds include the White and Gray Call, Black East India, Wood Duck, Mandarin, and Teal. If you're looking for a more utilitarian breed, try Muscovy or Rouen. Both are good foragers and will be right at home free-ranging on your acreage. A 10-day-old pedigreed Muscovy duckling costs around U.S. $15. For a breed that grows quickly and produces a fair amount of eggs, the Pekin is a common favorite. The commercial duck industry relies heavily on this variety of duck for its egg production. A hatchling Pekin can cost as little as U.S. $5.

RAISE HATCHLINGS Ducklings can be raised similarly to chicks, but because they grow faster, you'll need to keep them in a place where you can incrementally increase their floor space. As long as the ducklings are out of the weather and in a dry, decently lit, and ventilated place, most any building can serve as a good brooding area. Use 4 inches (10 cm) or so of an absorbent litter material like peat moss or wood shavings. Add new litter material often, removing any wet spots as they present themselves. Ducks are more susceptible to litter dampness issues than chicks. Make sure the waterer isn't big enough for the ducks to climb into.

KEEP DUCKLINGS WARM An infrared heat lamp is a convenient and good source of warmth for your ducklings. You'll need one. If your ducklings are staying away from the lamp, that's a good indicator it's too hot. Similarly, if the ducklings are clamoring and piling toward the center of the lamp's rays, you probably need to kick up the heat a little. One of the biggest benefits of raising ducks is their hardiness. They aren't susceptible to many of the common poultry illnesses. This means you probably won't need medicated feeds. Instead, look for a supplier in your area that carries duck feed. If you can't find specific food for ducks, chick starter will work for the first few weeks. Then ducklings can be transitioned to eating a pelleted chicken grower ration with cracked corn or grain.

100

BAKE BETTER CAKES WITH DUCK EGGS

DUCK EGGS, A BAKER'S DELIGHT Hold a duck egg in your hand and you can feel how much bigger and heavier it is than a chicken egg. Duck eggs are prized for Asian dishes, such as salted duck eggs. And bakers and chefs love the richer, deeper flavor of duck eggs over those of chicken eggs in baking. Give cake batter a thicker consistency by substituting chicken eggs with duck eggs. The extra protein and yolk in the duck egg thicken the batter without changing any other ingredients.

BEST EGG LAYERS The best duck breeds for duck eggs are typically smaller, leaner birds. The right breed will convert feed energy into egg production instead of gaining weight. Many of the best duck breeds for eggs have also had the broody trait bred out of them, meaning they are less inclined to stop laying in order to incubate their eggs. Examples include the Khaki Campbell duck, a brown domestic duck that originated in England, and the Runner duck. Both breeds lay eggs at a rate that certainly challenges the laying rate of chickens!

101

ENJOY THE OTHER DARK MEAT

The best duck breeds for meat are those that efficiently convert feed energy into rapid weight gains.

Pekins are large white ducks with orange beaks; they look like the quintessential farm duck found in elementary school picture books. Most of the duck meat eaten in this country is from Pekin ducks; it is typically the breed found on commercial duck farms.

Rouen is slower growing than the Pekin, but it reaches the same weight over the 5- to 6-month period of feeding and foraging under farm flock conditions.

Muscovy ducks have become popular on small farms. They have lean, nutritious meat that is comparable in taste to sirloin steak. Muscovy ducks are also prolific egg layers, producing up to 180 eggs per year.

102

GET HOPPING WITH RABBITS

If you're considering adding rabbits to your acreage, first decide why you want to raise them: pets, show animals, meat (for yourself or to sell), breeding, fiber, or a combination of these. Research the different rabbit breeds and choose based on your goals. If you have questions, it's a good idea to attend a rabbit show and talk to breeders and owners of several different breeds. Learn about food and housing requirements before you bring your bunnies home.

RABBITS AS PETS Rabbits can make wonderful pets, and many have a lifespan of 10 years or more. You'll need to set up a cage and might also want to get a few baby gates to keep the bunnies where they belong if you raise them in the house. Some rabbits can even be trained to use a litter box! Keep in mind rabbits are social creatures, so they may be happier if you have at least two. If you are keeping rabbits as pets and aren't interested in breeding them, they can be spayed or neutered just like a dog or cat. You'll want to keep them in their cage when you aren't home because they do have a tendency to chew on things like electrical cords. Some rabbits have temperaments similar to cats and will snuggle on your lap.

SHOWING RABBITS Rabbits are a good alternative for children who are interested in showing animals through 4-H or at county fairs. Rabbits are easy to safely handle and don't require a lot of space that larger livestock such as sheep and cattle need. Rabbit shows are held all around the country for owners of all ages.

RABBIT FIBER You may think sheep or goats are the only animals you can raise for fiber, but Angora rabbits take less space and are easier for children to handle. They can be brushed daily, and the fur collected, and they can be sheared once every 90 days or so. Their wool can bring anywhere from U.S. $5 to $15 per ounce (28 g), depending on the quality and color.

RAISING MEAT Raising meat rabbits can be a way to feed your family a healthy and sustainable protein as well as to become a profitable business venture. Rabbits are known for their ability to multiply. Two does (female rabbits) and two bucks (male rabbits) will produce 40 to 50 rabbits a year. Rabbit meat breeds include New Zealand White, Californian, and American.

103

RAISE PASTURE RABBITS FOR MEAT

If you raise rabbits, put them out on pasture so they can have all the fresh greens they want. Keep them in a wire cage on the ground and move it at least once a day. They'll eat just about anything, but alfalfa is high in protein.

Rabbits raised on pasture in a rotational grazing system produce quality meat higher in omega-3 fatty acids. Another benefit is the savings in feed costs. But it also depends on your objectives and how fast you want them to grow.

If you're trying to do things with the least amount of cost possible, they can get a fair amount of their diet from just pasture in the summertime. If you want them to grow faster, feed them pellets.

One thing all rabbits do quickly is dig holes. To keep them from escaping, you can put a floor in the cage. But it has to be constructed so the bunnies can still nibble the grass the way they prefer. Rabbits like to eat the grass from the tip down. When it's bent over, they don't seem to like it as much.

Have electric fencing around the cages to discourage any predators looking for a rabbit dinner.

104

BUILD A BETTER HUTCH

Whether you have rabbits as pets or for commercial use, they need a hutch to live in. Rabbits that live outside can take the cold, but not drafts. They're prone to respiratory illnesses, so if you're building a hutch, keep this in mind.

PROTECT FROM WEATHER A hutch should have a solid roof with overhangs for protection from the weather. Your rabbits will need a warm place to stay during the winter. If you can move their hutch into a garage or barn, that's probably a good idea. Give them a nice blanket of hay to snuggle up in, and they'll be fine.

USE THE RIGHT WOOD Rabbits like to chew; if the wood has a lot of knots or edges, the rabbits sink their teeth into it. So it's best to use smooth, solid wood for the sides.

GIVE THEM SPACE Each bunny needs its own living quarters. If the rabbits are full-grown, it's not a good idea to have many of them in one hutch. Mature bucks may fight. Small breeds need about a 2×3 feet (61× 92 cm) of space, and larger breeds should have a hutch that measures at least 2×4 feet (61 cm × 1.2 m).

KEEP PREDATORS AT BAY To protect rabbits from predators, hutches should be up off the ground a couple of feet (60 cm) or so.

105

ADD SHEEP TO YOUR ACREAGE

LAND You can graze about five or six ewes per acre in a well-managed, continuously grazed pasture.

BUILDINGS Housing needs vary by climate, lambing season, and individual preferences. More elaborate housing is generally required if lambing will occur during periods of inclement weather. Simple shelters may be adequate if lambing will occur on pasture during periods of mild weather.

Old dairy and hog barns make good shelter, and many facilities can be remodeled to accommodate sheep. Understand that sheep should have an open, cold, dry barn rather than a tight, warm, humid barn. They wear thick coats and generally do well in the cold.

EQUIPMENT While sheep aren't extremely needy, they do require some general maintenance, and it's important to be sure you have the equipment necessary to tend to them. You will need tools for shearing, foot trimming, tail docking, and ear tagging, as well as proper fencing, sorting and lambing pens, and corrals. Additional standard maintenance includes cleaning the barns and harvesting hay (or being prepared to pay for it).

NUTRITION Sheep are ruminants, which means they have a four-compartment stomach and live off of grass and hay. They can use the high-fiber diet and digest it because of the bacteria that live in their stomachs. While sheep are typically sustained by hay or grass, it is sometimes necessary to feed them grain, such as corn, for energy. Situations such as late pregnancy, lactation, and rapid-growing lambs require such nutritional attention

106

BUILD A SHEEP'S MILK DAIRY FLOCK

Feta, pecorino, and ricotta are just a few of the cheeses that are made from sheep milk. Popular in nearly every country, these delicious cheeses can be made from the sheep you milk yourself.

THE GLORIES OF SHEEP MILK Sheep milk is rich in fat, solids, and minerals. This makes it ideal for making cheese and yogurt, plus spa items, such as soap and lotion. Sheep milk is also lower in lactose than cow's milk, making it more palatable for consumers who are lactose-intolerant.

MILKING BREEDS There are sheep breeds specifically bred for milk production; they include the Lacaune and East Friesian. The East Friesian have the highest milk production and is the breed mostly often used in the United States for dairy sheep.

MILKING FACILITIES You'll need a barn or shed that can comfortably accommodate ewes and their lambs. Setting up a small milking parlor for sheep isn't much different than for goats or cattle except for the attachment sizes.

DAIRY FLOCK MAINTENANCE In dairy flocks, lambs are weaned at around 30 days old. This allows the producer to have the ewes in the milking parlor while they're still producing adequate amounts of milk. At peak production, ewes will give 1 to 2 gallons (3.75–7.5 L) of milk per day.

107

DISCOVER THE DIFFERENCE BETWEEN SHEEP AND GOATS

Goats are browsers and sheep are grazers. Browsers like to eat leaves, bark, and the stems of plants, including those that grow vertically, such as trees and shrubs. Grazers eat plants at the ground level. Goats look up for food. Sheep look down. Notice how in this photo the goats are standing on a shed roof so they can reach tree leaves? Sheep would never attempt such a high-wire act for food.

108

WORK WITH A
SHEEP SHEARER

Finding a professional to shear a flock of sheep these days can be difficult. Sheep shearers have become a rare commodity because the number of sheep has gone down in the U.S. For professionals to make a living, it's all about volume, and many shearers can't justify the time to travel and set up their equipment for a small flock. But for those with small flocks, there are strategies:

COMMINGLE FLOCKS Combine flocks with neighbors so that the shearer can have a bigger volume in one visit.

TAKE THE SHEEP TO THE SHEARER If you have a really small flock–say, four or five sheep–you can haul the sheep to the shearer instead of the shearer coming to you. Or if they're going to be shearing someplace close, bring them to that location and shear them there (with your neighbor's permission, of course).

DON'T TRY IT YOURSELF Sheep shearing involves a lot more than just giving the sheep a trim. The right shearing equipment costs hundreds of dollars. And if you don't know what you're doing, you can harm the animal. It's very important that the person with the blades knows how to handle the sheep.

OFFER SOME HELP It takes at least two other people helping the shearer. While the shearer is working, one person has the next ewe ready to go and the other is bagging up the wool. It takes between 3 and 5 minutes to shear a sheep.

SHEARING COSTS Depending on your area, the shearer will either charge a flat fee for the whole herd or a charge per head. Find a professional to shear your sheep through the American Sheep Industry Association.

109

SELL YOUR WOOL

You may be able to spin a profit from wool production. When the sheep are sheared every spring, all that wool has to go somewhere. You might as well try to sell it. There are plenty of wool crafters and fiber manufacturers looking for good-quality fleece. Here are some tips for selling wool:

MAKE SURE IT'S CLEAN You want to keep as much vegetable matter, such as hay, straw, and grass, out of the fibers. Also trim off fleece stained with manure.

LONG FIBERS ARE BEST Wool buyers are looking for fleeces that are approximately 3 to 3½ inches (8–9 cm) long. That's called "staple length." It's what the commercial machinery and factories are made to work with.

KEEP WOOL DRY Make sure the wool is dry when it's sheared and also when it goes into the bag. Don't store wool in a black garbage bag because the wool will sweat. Burlap and specialty plastic bags developed for the wool industry are preferred.

COLOR MATTERS Wool is graded and priced per pound (.5 kg), depending on the quality of the fiber and the animal it comes from. Black-face breeds bring less money from commercial sources because

they usually have black fiber in their wool. Black fiber does not take dye, so there is a deduction in the U.S. 35- to 45-cent range. White-face breeds with a medium white-face wool get U.S. 60 to 65 cents a pound. Rambouillets and Merinos with the high-quality fine wool will bring U.S. $1.25 or more.

MARKET YOUR WOOL Handspinners and knitters are a specialty market for your wool, especially if you have unusual breeds of sheep and varied-color fleeces. Selling your wool on-farm or at a fiber-related show allows you to market directly to individuals who are looking for specialty fleeces. Your sheep shearer may also be a good source of information on who's buying wool in your area.

110

RAISE DAIRY GOATS FOR MILK AND CHEESE

One or two goats can furnish fresh milk for a family on a year-round basis. Goat milk is known to have more easily digestible fat and protein contents than cow milk. Some dairy goats can average 6 to 8 pounds (2.75–3.5 kg) of milk a day (roughly 3 to 4 quarts) (3–3.75 L) during their lactation periods. Surplus milk can be used for butter or cheese or to raise other young animals.

If you plan to keep a dairy goat for family milk, you should be certain the animal is tested and is free of disease. A local veterinarian can help you with this.

Some communities have zoning laws or ordinances that prohibit goats and other animals in urban areas. Check the regulations for your area.

DAIRY GOAT BREEDS

There are five main breeds of dairy goats: Toggenburg, Saanen, Nubian, Alpine, and American La Mancha.

Certain characteristics are stronger in some breeds than others. Toggenburgs are recognized for long lactations, with fat content of milk averaging 3.8 percent. Saanens are larger goats and are recognized for being heavy milkers, with 3.5 percent fat average. The smaller Nubians are noted for higher milk fat than the other breeds. Alpines are recognized as a hardy breed and milk well, producing about 3.5 percent fat milk. A characteristic of the La Mancha breed is no visible external ears. They are large animals and good milkers with milk at about 4 percent fat. Angora and pygmy goats are not good milk animals.

BUYING A GOOD MILKER

If you want to supply family milk, good grade or nonregistered goats will serve this purpose. For a variety of reasons, you may prefer to buy registered, pedigreed animals, but the cost will be higher. If your goal is milk, your chief concern will be the milking production of the goat. Total milk production depends on the amount of milk daily and how long the doe will produce before going dry.

A good milker will produce an average of 2½ to 3 quarts (2–3 L) daily over a period of 9 to 10 months. Such goats may produce up to 1½ gallons (5.5 L) daily during the peak period of lactation and between 1 and 2 quarts (0.9–1.9 L) later in the lactation. Two goats, bred to freshen 3 to 4 months apart, should ensure some milk every day of the year.

If you want your goats to also clean up weeds, remember that some plants may give milk an off-flavor.

DISCOVER DELIGHTFUL GOATS

For milk, meat, fiber, pets, and for general yard grass maintenance, goats make a great utility breed for any homestead.

ALPINE This dairy breed originated in the French Alps. They are the highest-producing milkers, with top goats producing up to 2 gallons (7.5 L) per day.

LA MANCHA La Mancha goats produce milk with high protein and butterfat content. This breed can be milked for two years after giving birth.

NUBIAN Nubians sport long, floppy ears and a convex "Roman nose" muzzle. This breed can thrive in hotter climates than other dairy goats. Raised for meat and dairy.

SAANEN Saanen goats are the largest breed of dairy goat and are second in milk production only to Alpine goats. They have an easy-going temperament.

BOER Originally bred in South Africa, Boers are now one of the principal meat goat breeds in the United States.

SPANISH These meat goats are excellent foragers and will climb a tree for the last leaf. They're good mothers, easy birthers, hardy, and resistant to many parasites.

KIKO This meat goat from New Zealand is easy to raise, grows to market weight quickly, and will even clean up weeds on your acreage.

TENNESSEE FAINTING (MYOTONIC) Indigenous to the United States, these goats don't actually faint but stiffen or tense up when startled or excited. They make great pets.

PYGMY An adult pygmy goat is about as big as a medium-size dog, which makes these mini goats perfect for acreages. While this breed does produce milk, they are most often raised as pets and for show.

NIGERIAN DWARF This small dairy breed has big personality! They are often used for showing as well.

ANGORA Angora goats produce mohair, often used in making sweaters, scarves, and other garments.

CASHMERE Goats raised for cashmere have been selectively bred to produce high-quality fiber. It takes four goats about a year to produce enough cashmere for a sweater.

112

GIVE THEM SHELTER

Goats don't need a fancy place to live, but they need to be protected from the rain, wind, and cold. Keep your goats happy and healthy by providing shelter in their pen or out in the pasture. Goats should be housed in a shed or barn, with access to the outdoors. Ideally, each goat should have at least 20 to 25 square feet (2–2.35 sq m) of indoor space, 0.2-0.3 acres (.8–1.2 ha) of pasture with an exercise area of 50 square feet (5 sq m).

MOVEABLE HUTS Three-sided huts allow plenty of air movement and can be moved around so the opening is facing away from direct

wind. Be sure there is plenty of space for the goats to hunker down, whether that's several small shelters or one big one. It's good to give bucks a little bit more room. The shelter should be tall enough to

provide sufficient headroom for the goat to stand upright on its hind legs with its neck outstretched. When lying down, goats appreciate a soft, dry bed of sawdust, wood chips, or straw.

113

LEARN MORE ABOUT GOATS

Goats have quirky personalities and are an efficient source of meat and milk. But there are other reasons to add goats to your homestead.

GOATS ARE WEED EATERS If you have a lot of brush and weeds to clear from your property, set free some goats. They'll clear your land faster than any weed whacker can.

It generally takes 60 goats three to five days to clear about a quarter of an acre (0.1 ha) of relatively dense vegetation.

GOATS ARE SMART Some studies show that goats are as smart as dogs.

They live in social groups, can puzzle out how to get to hard-to-reach foods, and they live for 15 to 18 years, so they are able to develop skills that shorter-lived animals can't.

GOATS HAVE INTERESTING EYES A goat's pupils are rectangular. This gives them vision for about 340 degrees around without ever having to move. Goats also have great night vision.

GOATS HAVE THEIR OWN VOCABULARY Buck is a male goat. Doe is a female goat. Buckling is a baby male goat. Doeling is a baby female goat. Chevon is goat meat. A herd, tribe, or trip is a group of goats that lives together.

114

GET—AND KEEP—GOATS

Anyone who raises goats has chased down these clever escape artists. Here are some ideas for keeping goats contained:

DISCOURAGE JUMPERS Most goats are very nimble, so you need fences high enough to keep them from jumping over. A board fence will work fine as long as it is at least 4 feet (1.2 m) tall.

THINK VERTICAL Since goats love to climb, another option is fencing with vertical bars so the goats can't stand on them.

KEEP ELECTRIC FENCES ON String an electric wire parallel to anything a goat sees as a challenge to jump over. After the first zap or two, most goats will respect it with no problem. But smart goats are very good at noticing when you unplug the fence and there's no electricity flowing through the wire. So keep electric fence hot.

CONSIDER HORNED SPECIES If using a woven-wire fence with goats with horns, they tend to get their heads stuck in the fence. Put one strand of an electric wire on the inside of the fence to keep them from pushing up against the woven-wire fence.

115

FENCE THEM IN WITH WIRE OR VINYL

Consider these other fencing options based on your livestock needs:

WIRE Barbed wire is used for large stock, such as cows and horses. Woven wire restrains smaller animals such as sheep. Or use a combination of woven wire on the bottom and one or more strands of barbed wire on top. Use wood or steel posts with wire. Corner posts need to be braced and wires need to be tight. Construction costs for a commercially installed woven and barbed wire fence range from U.S. 90¢ to $2.50 per foot (30 cm), depending on spacing, posts, and the kind and number of wires.

HIGH TENSILE WIRE High-tensile wire fences are less expensive to install than traditional wire fences. Wires are tightened onto posts with a small winch. Construction costs will run from U.S. 25¢ for a single wire on wide post spacing to U.S. $3 per foot for nine wires (three hot on one side and four hot on the other). You can put in a high-tensile fence for U.S. $1 to $1.50 per foot (30 cm), depending on post spacing.

VINYL Vinyl is attractive and a good fence option for horses. These are the most expensive fences, but have a long life. About U.S. $5 to $7 per foot (30 cm) will get you a standard three-board vinyl fence.

116

USE LLAMAS AS PREDATOR CONTROL

To prevent the predation of their flocks by wild animals, many small livestock producers have turned to guard llamas. Llamas have an instinctual fear of canines and canine-like animals from their ancestors being hunted by mountain lions and wild dogs. Llamas in South America are the natural prey of these key predators.

Because dogs and coyotes are among the greatest predators of sheep, a llama can be very effective in alerting and protecting a flock against such predators. A good guard llama will usually charge them, and if the predator does not retreat, kick and stomp them.

Llamas work best singly among their flock of sheep. One llama is capable of guarding up to 2,000 sheep in up to 300 acres (121 ha) and can decrease the amount of predation in a flock up to 100 percent.

A single llama can be used to guard a flock for 10 to 20 years. Llamas eat the same food as sheep, use the same vaccines, and adjust to guarding their sheep within hours or days of introduction to the flock. Llamas can be halter-broken.

117

LEARN THE SHOCKING TRUTH ABOUT THE ELECTRIC FENCE

Whether attempting to keep livestock in or deer out, nothing works as effectively as electric fencing. Electric fences deliver a strong but relatively harmless electrical shock using high voltage and low amperage.

PROTECT FENCES Including one or more hot, or electrified, wires on a fence helps it last longer and requires less maintenance because animals are deterred from rubbing on them. They also allow animals to be more easily contained during active periods, such as breeding and weaning.

CHOOSE MANY OPTIONS Electric fence comes in temporary, semi-permanent, and permanent options. Temporary fences are easy to move; semi-permanent fences serve in the interim until a permanent fence can be installed; and a permanent fence isn't intended to be moved for a number of years.

INTRODUCING ANIMALS For animals to respect a fence, they must recognize it as a barrier. Train them to the fence first. Contained animals can be trained by placing a short working sample inside the corral.

POULTRY FENCING Electrified netting is the best way to contain pasturing poultry because it is extremely easy to install, adjust, and remove; it's perfect for rotating them to fresh grass. Line posts are generally built into the net, and no tools are needed. Simply unroll the netting, push in the line posts (by hand or foot), join the separate rolls, push in the end and corner posts (by hand or foot), and connect to the energizer. The netting is hand-tensioned, easily adapting to curves and hills. Closely spaced vertical lengths and energized horizontal lengths combine to create both a physical and pain barrier for birds and predators. A more permanent netting option uses stronger posts spaced closer together. This reduces sagging, a common problem in net fences, but is more difficult to install and remove.

SHEEP FENCING Electrified netting is a good option for containing sheep. While most will be contained by a fence reaching about 35 inches (88 cm) in height, larger and more rambunctious sheep will need a taller option at about 42 inches (107 cm) high. Many manufacturers offer net fencing in prefabricated rolls, complete with struts and posts, making it easy to install and remove. When installed, the result is a nearly impenetrable mesh of energized strands to keep sheep in and predators, such as coyotes and dogs, out. A five-strand rope or twine fence is cheaper, but netting protects better against predators. The best way to permanently manage sheep, while deterring predators, is with the use of a woven high-tensile wire fence and offset charged wires or rope. The woven wire should reach about 32 inches (81 cm) tall and be attached to the nongrazed side of the fence if there is one. Two or more high-tensile wires are attached above this for additional height, and up to two charged strands of rope or wire are offset on the grazed sides. To supplement the woven wire, one strand of barbed wire set along the bottom discourages coyotes and dogs from digging under the fence.

CHAPTER 6

Indoors: Live Naturally & Beautifully

Putting the "home" in "homestead" is a matter of creating a warm, cozy, and inviting interior living space. If you are drawn to the country–where Nature carpets the ground in green and growing things and the elements act on everything they touch–it's likely you are taken with patinas, rustic furnishings, vintage pieces, and home care products that are as pure and natural as possible. Here are a few ideas and projects for making your home as enticing as the land on which it sits.

118

HANG IT UP

Predrill holes, then screw flea market-found vintage doorknobs along with one-off cabinet and furniture hardware into a piece of salvaged wood to create a rustic entry organizer for keys, bags, and outerwear.

119

STORE SMART IN YOUR MUDROOM

Hats, coats, backpacks, boots, shoes, umbrellas, and pet gear: There's a lot that happens in your mudroom, and organization can quickly get away from you. Fortunately, a few clever ideas help you to take advantage of every square inch and keep your mudroom necessities stored in good order.

ESTABLISH A MUDROOM ZONE Even homes with grand entries (and often in older homes) sometimes find themselves challenged by the lack of front- or backdoor space to store daily necessities. A few options can help. Consider a bench with storage space under the lid or a drawer underneath that offers a spot to stash seasonal items. If there's no room for individual shoe storage, place boots and other foot gear on a tray to catch moisture and loose dirt.

USE BASKETS FOR OUTDOOR ITEMS It makes sense to have some items close at hand for out-of-house comings and goings. A shelf above coat storage can offer space for containers with items such as sunscreen, bandages, and more. Keep similar items, such as bug spray, together and label containers (adhesive or tied-on tags work well).

TUCK SHOES OUT OF THE WAY Although it's handy to have all mudroom storage together, sometimes it's not feasible. Instead,

carve out nooks and crannies where you can. A small recessed area can provide a just-right spot for multiple shoe shelves–and it will be out of sight.

Sliding shelves are a useful tool in mudrooms, too, helping to streamline access to items. Choose heavy-duty, easy-to-clean surfaces in a mudroom, particularly for the floor–which takes hard use–that rely on color and texture to mask any messes and daily dirt.

USE EXTRA STORAGE FOR ESSENTIALS Some mudrooms are big enough to store more than just coats and shoes. It's very handy to have your washer and dryer in the mudroom for quick strip-and-wash operations involving muddy clothes. Store cleaning supplies and other items such as thermoses on shelving. For peculiarly shaped items that may not easily stay grouped–rags, for example–use baskets to keep them in order.

120

RECLAIM WOOD

Mellow, rich in character, and in demand, salvaged wood is now widely available and affordable.

Here's how to shop for wood that works and is safe for your family:

BUY FROM THE BEST Beware of sellers trying to make a quick buck from salvaged wood. Look for established dealers who guarantee their product and whose prices are in line with the average market price.

MAKE SURE IT'S MILLED Weathered old wood has its inconsistencies, which is why it needs millwork, especially if used in interiors. Ask the seller if the wood has been trimmed from a larger piece and planed and if all old nails have been removed.

KILN DRYING IS KEY Old wood contains moisture. To prevent warping, the material should be kiln-dried. This drying process also will curtail any infestations, ensuring you won't bring termites or other wood-boring insects into your home.

121

LIGHT UP YOUR LIFE

Interior designers often say lighting is to a room what jewelry is to an outfit–the finishing touch. Make a statement and save cash by converting dome and cylindrical industrial finds–such as this black metal basket, copper tin, and metal strainer–into illuminating decor with pendant light kits. Use a large drill bit to create a hole in each object wide enough to thread the wiring through, and it's lights on.

122

MAKE A WOOD WINE RACK

After a long day of pulling weeds in the garden or wrangling goats, taking a long, hot shower and relaxing on the porch with a glass of wine to watch the sun set over your little acreage is one of the joys of living in the country. Be sure you always have your favorite libation on hand with a rustic wine rack made from reclaimed wood (see #120). It can be done in just a couple of hours—leaving you plenty of time to sit, sip, and be glad you live where you do.

MATERIALS
Barnwood cut to 5¼×2×21¾ inches (13.25×5×55.25 cm); measuring tape; drill press (or scrap wood; 1¼-inch [3.25 cm] spade bit, and clamp); drill; handsaw; ¼-inch (6 mm) and ⅝-inch (2 cm) drill bits

STEP 3 Measure 1½ inches (3.75 cm) from the top and bottom of the rack and cut away all but ¾ inch (2 cm) with a handsaw to create tabs for hanging. Drill a ¼-inch (19 mm) hole, centered in each tab. Lightly sand edges.

STEP 1 Mark the centers of four holes along the wood block, spaced every 4½ inches (11.5 cm).

STEP 2 If you don't have a drill press, cut a scrap piece of wood with a 7-degree angle and clamp it on top of the wine rack to use it as a guide as you drill the hole using a drill and spade bit. The angle is important to keep bottles inserted.

STEP 4 Mount the rack into a wall stud if possible. Use a stud finder to locate the stud; mark holes for the screws at the desired height. Drill holes using the ⅝-inch (20 mm) bit and install the rack with 2-inch (5 cm) screws. If you can't install the rack into a stud, use a tape measure and level to mark holes for the screws. Drill holes using a ⅝-inch (20 mm) bit, add plastic toggle anchors with a hammer, and attach the rack with 2-inch (5 cm) screws into the anchors. Make sure the holes along the wine rack are angled upward when installed.

123

TAKE YOUR PLACES

Who says dishes have to match?
Set a delightful table by mixing
found treasures. If desired,
choose one color for the base
plate to unify. Or opt for plates
within the same color family.
For example, cobalt, cornflower,
and pale seafoam harmonize
beautifully here.

124

MIX POTPOURRI FROM THE GARDEN

Extend your gardening enjoyment and bring the color, fragrance, and texture of nature into your home by mixing a batch of potpourri.

CREATIVE COMPOSITION Potpourri is a mixture of botanicals, or flowers and leaves, and fruit. Included in the mix are what many herbalists call "gatherings." These are heavier items such as rose hips, cinnamon sticks, and orange-peel ribbons that add texture as well as a secondary scent to the mixture.

A fragrant potpourri oil such as lavender, rose, or eucalyptus is often added to the dry mix. In a potpourri oil, the base scent, rose, for instance, is mixed with a carrier, such as sweet almond oil. The neutral carrier oil stretches the expensive essential oil without adding an overpowering scent of its own.

MULTIPLE USES A bowl of potpourri is more than a nose-pleasing mix. It serves the same purpose in a room as a vase of fragrant cut flowers–adding color and interest–but will last for 3 to 6 months.

In an enclosed space, the scent will last even longer: Fill a fabric bag with potpourri or tie some in a handkerchief, and you have a sachet that can be put in a drawer to scent clothes or bedding for many months.

STEP-BY-STEP POTPOURRI

STEP 1 Slice fruit and spread it out to dry. Make thin slices. Orange slices will take about 2 weeks to dry in the open air. Use a mesh surface or rack so air flows around the slices. Keeping the slices in the oven with the heat turned off will keep insects away. A gas oven with a pilot light will cut drying time. A dehydrator will dry fruit in about 8 hours.

STEP 2 Select and prepare flowers and leaves for drying. Trim the material into manageable pieces, leaving stems long enough so you can bundle several with a rubber band. As the material dries and shrinks, the rubber band will tighten. Hang the bundles from a beam with a length of raffia to dry. Open-air drying will take about 2 weeks.

STEP 3 When all the ingredients are dried and cut into smaller pieces, they are ready to be mixed by hand in a bowl. Be sure to store unused material in sealable plastic bags or Mason jars for future use. Some fruits, such as apple slices, may turn dark but will still be usable.

STEP 4 After the botanicals are mixed to the desired color combination, add potpourri oil for a more potent scent. Use 6 to 10 drops of oil for a medium-size bowl of potpourri, then gently but thoroughly mix the potpourri. Choose an oil that will enhance the botanicals.

125

PRETTY UP WITH PIE TINS

A tin pie pan is as American as apple pie, so instead of hiding history in a cupboard, bring it out in the open to add interest to a kitchen wall. In production for more than 100 years, the tins come in plenty of styles. At flea markets, older handmade examples and hammered or punched pans claim the highest prices.

126

FRAME YOUR GARDEN MEMORIES

Drying and pressing flowers is a favorite activity of gardeners and foragers alike, but what do you do with them? Make a collage! But first, you need dried flowers and other botanical materials.

PRESSING FLOWERS

Lay flowers or leaves facedown on smooth, absorbent paper such as white blotter paper. Build layers of plant materials between sandwiches of paper.

Use a press or make one from two rectangles of plywood with four holes drilled near the corners. Use wing nuts from a hardware store to tighten. Or press materials between pages of a heavy book with more weight piled on top.

If you are using a flower press, retighten wing nuts after two days (as water in the flowers is absorbed by the paper, the press loosens).

To keep colors bright, after about four days carefully remove flowers and leaves with tweezers and lay

them on dry paper to continue the pressing process. Use the tip of a small paring knife to loosen if necessary. If you're using a book, change pages of the book.

AIR-DRYING FLOWERS

Bunch a small cluster of stems with a rubber band. Hang upside down in a warm, dark, dry place.

For small items, such as marigolds and rosebuds, place them on a cooling rack on a tray on top of your refrigerator. The warmth usually flows up from the back of the fridge and over the flowers to dry them quickly.

GATHER MATERIALS

Part of the fun of creation is in the hunt. Elements might include photos; colored papers cut from magazines or newspapers; packaging; seed packs; keepsakes; leftover crafts materials from other projects such as bits of fabric, yarn, ribbon, beads, or wire; and stuff from your junk drawer. You also can use pressed or air-dried flowers,

petals, leaves, pods, cones, and twigs–just about anything that isn't too heavy.

For the background, use corrugated cardboard, foam core, stretched canvas, or any other art boards available in an art supply or crafts store. You'll also need scissors and white glue, a glue stick, acrylic soft gel, glue gun, or gorilla glue.

ASSEMBLE YOUR COLLAGE

If necessary, cut background board to desired size. Cut or tear paper and lay on the board. Papers can also be folded, fringed, shredded, crunched, or pleated. Move the pieces around until you like the layout. Brush glue on paper and/ or botanical elements with a small paintbrush. If you're using colored tissue paper, spread glue on the board first and put the tissue paper on top of the glue. (Use the same technique for small seeds, beads, and fragile leaves.) As you paste down the paper, petals, or leaves, start at the center of each piece and gently press to the edges, squeezing out any air. Allow to dry.

127

CULTIVATE AFRICAN VIOLETS

African violets come in a rainbow of hues and brighten indoor spaces throughout the year with their velvety blossoms and fuzzy foliage when the flower garden is dormant or buried under a blanket of snow. But violets are more than a seasonal pick-me-up. With proper care, they can bloom continuously and live for decades. In fact, the oldest known violet–dubbed Superman by its original owner–is 58 years old and still going strong.

Violets are also easy to cultivate. They're simple to propagate by leaf cuttings, so you can easily and inexpensively add to your collection. True to their name, African violets were discovered in East Africa. While serving as governor of an African province in 1892, Baron Walter von Saint Paul found them growing on shady rock ledges and sent seeds home to Germany. By the early 1900s, violets were growing in homes throughout Europe. They arrived in the United States in the late 1920s when a Los Angeles nursery imported seeds from British greenhouses and hybridized 10 varieties–many of which are still grown.

Today's violets are even showier than the varieties our grandmothers grew. They've evolved into an array of colorations and more than 30,000 cultivars that bloom in nearly every hue, including pink, red, white, green, and even buttery yellow. Double, fringed, and "fantasy" blooms that boast splotches or streaks of multiple hues add even more intrigue to the mix. And variegated varieties prove that foliage can be as enchanting as the blooms.

STEP-BY-STEP PROPAGATION

STEP 1 It's a snap to start new African violets from cuttings: Using a sharp blade, cut a healthy leaf from the base of the stem. A long stem will work best.

STEP 2 Plant the cutting in a suitable rooting medium such as peat moss and sand. Use the end of a pencil to create a hole about 1 inch (2.5 cm) deep.

STEP 3 Insert the long, straight stem into the rooting mixture and gently tamp down the medium around it. Water well and place in a bright location.

STEP 4 Kept warm, the leaf will develop roots and new shoots from the base of the leafstalk. The rooted cutting will soon develop into a sturdy new plant.

128

MAKE A HAND-TIED BOUQUET

Practice your farmer-florist skills with a "perfect" flower recipe to fashion a lush, fun, seasonal bouquet. The design technique works with a variety of flowers. Good cut-flower choices include cosmos, sunflower, coneflower, zinnia, pin cushion flower, dahlia, and peegee hydrangea. Use this project as a guide, but feel free to substitute flowers and foliage from your own garden.

Above all, the choice of flowers and other plant materials for any arrangement depends on what is available. Think of seasonal bouquets as small paintings or photographs that capture vignettes of the garden in spring, summer, or fall.

FOCAL FLOWER Dahlia, peony, rose, or other dramatic bloom

DISK FLOWERS A smaller flower, equally eye-catching, to provide a chunk of color to the bouquet

FOLIAGE Herbs, soft greenery, or green flowers, such as bells of Ireland

FILLERS Soft textural elements, such as milkweed (*Asclepias* spp.)

SPIKES Strong vertical elements, such as snapdragons or lobelia

AIRY BITS Wispy, fluid element, such as Queen Anne's lace, nigella, goldenrod (*Solidago* spp.), or annual flaxseed heads

STEP 1 Hold one or two focal flowers in one hand and arrange with the other. These will become the center of the design. This bouquet starts with two stems of crested celosia.

STEP 2 Working in a circle as you rotate, add layers of elements by crossing the stems. Here, the foliage is bells of Ireland, the filler is milkweed (*Asclepias* spp.), and the new focal flower is a red dahlia.

STEP 3 Continue to rotate the bouquet, layering one more round of foliage, filler, and disk flowers (the smaller dahlias). Here, snapdragons and lobelia serve as the spike elements. Insert from the top and pull them into place to emerge above the other flowers.

STEP 4 Add airy elements, including annual flaxseed heads, to give the bouquet a little "twinkle." Note that the stems are symmetrically spiraled out and how the bouquet is gently held at its base.

STEP 5 Add other airy elements, such as Queen Anne's lace, nigella seedpods, and goldenrod, to lend a finishing touch. Add these before securely tying the bouquet with twine and finishing it with decorative ribbon.

129

FRESHEN UP WITH HERBS

If you have an herb garden–or even a few pots of herbs–you can create your own refreshing spa products.

HERBAL HAIR RINSE (A) Rosemary brings out the natural highlights in hair and is great for the scalp. Place a large handful of fresh rosemary, sage, and/or chamomile in a 1-quart (1 L) jar and pour 2 cups (500 ml) boiling water over the herbs. Cover loosely with a lid or saucer, and steep for 10 to 15 minutes. Allow the infusion to cool. Strain and discard herbs. To use, shampoo your hair, then pour the cooled infusion over rinsed hair. Do not rinse out.

HERBAL SPRITZ (B) Fill a 1-quart (1 L) jar with your favorite herbs, such as mint, lavender, rosemary, lemon balm, and rose petals. Cover with apple cider vinegar. Let steep for several days; strain out the solids and pour the herb-infused vinegar into an atomizer or spray bottle. Keep the spritz in the refrigerator for an extra-cooling effect. Spray on your arms, legs, and face.

PEPPERMINT FOOT SOAK (C) Thanks to the prolific growth habit of mint, you can enjoy a foot soak often during growing season. Bring 8 cups (2 L) water to boiling in a large pot; remove from heat. Add 4 cups (100 g) loosely packed fresh peppermint; cover with lid and steep for 15 minutes. Transfer the infusion to a basin. Add enough warm or cool water to make a comfortable footbath. Soak your feet in the footbath for at least 10 minutes.

SOOTHING LINIMENT (D) Create a calendula-infused oil for dry skin or massage. In an 8-ounce (250 ml) glass jar combine 1 cup (250 ml) fresh calendula petals and 1 cup (250 ml) olive or almond oil. Allow petals to steep oil for 1 week. Strain, pressing petals with the back of a spoon. Pour the oil back into the jar and discard the petals. Refrigerate the infused oil for up to 1 month.

A

B

C

D

130

MAKE YOUR OWN SOAP

MATERIALS

Block of glycerin (250–500 g), saucepan, Pyrex jug, plastic or metal spoon, natural dyes for soapmaking, plastic molds or plastic loaf pan, eyedropper, sharp knife, essential oil (optional)

STEP 1 Half-fill a saucepan with water, bring to boiling, then let it simmer. Cut the glycerin into chunks, place in the jug, and set the jug in the pan. Stir the glycerin while it melts, then remove from heat.

STEP 2 Use an eye-dropper to add dye(s) until you get the color you wish. Add 2 to 3 ml (or 1 teaspoon per 250 g glycerin) essential oil. Work quickly before the glycerin sets. If it sets too soon, remelt it. Pour into molds or plastic loaf pan. Let set for 24 hours. Pop soap out of molds. If using a loaf pan, remove from pan and cut into bars with a sharp knife.

TIP Add ingredients such as oatmeal and a teaspoon of honey to make a gorgeous oatmeal soap. For a finer oatmeal consistency, blend in a food processor before adding to the glycerin mixture in Step 2.

131

CLEAN THE NATURAL WAY

TOILETS Mix ¹/₂ cup baking soda (150 g) and ¹/₄ cup white (60 ml) vinegar in the toilet. Allow to soak for at least 15 to 30 minutes, scrub, and flush.

GLASS CLEANER Combine 1 cup (250 ml) water, 1 tablespoon white vinegar, and 1 tablespoon rubbing alcohol in a spray bottle. Spray on glass and wipe clean with a dry cloth.

STOVE GRATES Make a paste with water, baking soda, and a little kosher salt. Dampen grates and apply the paste with a damp cloth or sponge, rub in to remove grease and food, and rinse clean.

CAST IRON Dampen a cast-iron pan, sprinkle kosher salt in the bottom, scrub with a scrub brush, rinse clean, and dry thoroughly.

SINKS Sprinkle baking soda in your sink with a squirt of dish soap, then scrub and rinse.

CARPET AND MATTRESSES Stubborn smells in carpet and mattresses just need a little sprinkle of baking soda. Let it sit for up to an hour and vacuum up.

GROUT Make a paste with 1 tablespoon of cream of tartar mixed with water or lemon juice. Apply with a scrub brush (grout and sinks) or a soft sponge for smooth surfaces.

DINGY DISHES Stains inside coffee and tea cups and silverware scrapes will disappear with a paste made from water and cream of tartar applied with a sponge or scrub brush.

CUTTING BOARDS Slice a lemon in half, sprinkle a little kosher salt on the lemon or board, and rub in the direction of the wood grain.

SOAP SCUM Halve a lemon; rub the fruit side of a lemon on any faucet

that has soap scum, rinse, and dry.

WHITE CLOTHING Soak dingy whites in ¹/₄ to ¹/₂ cup (60–125 ml) lemon juice with water and launder. Lemon juice can also be added to the washing machine instead of bleach to whiten and freshen up clothing.

132

ORGANIZE THE LAUNDRY ROOM

CAPTURE CLOTHESPINS Use lidded glass to hold clothespins, orphan items discovered in pockets, and sewing notions for quick garment repairs. Keep them corralled in a galvanized bin (photo, right).

LONELY SOCKS BOX It happens at least once every load: a sock comes up missing. Designate a plastic box or basket as the receptacle for socks that are missing their match.

LET IT ROLL Stock a small tiered cart with specialty cleaners for clothing and home. It can park alongside the washing machine and can also be rolled anywhere it's needed.

HUNG OUT TO DRY A drying rack and/or rolling clothing rack for delicates and handwash-only items is a must in any laundry room. In a tight space, choose a wall-mount version that collapses to just a few inches deep.

CREATE SPACE FOR FOLDING Front-loading washing and dryer units allow you to build a countertop above for folding laundry and housing essentials such as laundry soap, fabric softener, and bleach.

MAKE IT SEW EASY Keep a sewing kit right near the dryer so you can make mending repairs right when you notice them while you're folding or ironing clean clothes.

CHAPTER 7

Outdoor Projects

If you've been captivated by country living, it's probably due in large part to the quiet, fresh air, wide-open spaces, and the peace and proximity of Nature. You buy a little piece of land so you can be out on it–working it, growing things on it, communing with it. These out-of-doors projects and ideas will help you make the most of your little piece of paradise.

133

GET GLOWING

Finally, there's a use for all those mismatched glass lampshades you've saved: They make wonderful votive candle holders. Fill a galvanized plant tray (available at a garden center) with a blanket of sheet moss to serve as a soft green bed for candlelight. Insert the votive candles inside the upturned glass shades and place the display on a flat surface, where it can light up the night.

134

CREATE A KOI POND

There is nothing quite like the serene quality a koi pond brings to an outdoor space. Turn a plain patch of ground into a water garden with an international blend of plantings and brightly colored fish through the water.

Koi ponds can be as plain or as complicated as you like–from a simple pool of water to a body of water embellished with a waterfall surrounded by a footbridge, paths, boulders, statues, and lush plantings.

HOW TO BUILD Here is the basic process for creating your own koi pond. Keep in mind that Japanese koi need at least 2 square feet (60 sq cm) of pond surface by the time they are fully grown.

Plan for a pond surface area of 50 or more square feet (15.2 sq m) (such as an 8-foot–diameter [2.4-m] circle or a 5×10-foot rectangle [1.5×3-m] and a depth of 1½ to 2 feet (48 to 60 cm).

Line the sides and the bottom of the pond hole with 2 inches (5 cm) of wet sand. Top this with a polyvinyl chloride liner, extending the edges above ground. Use extra pond liner material, plus aquarium sealant and spray-foam insulation, to ensure a water-tight foundation.

WHERE TO BUILD Build the pond in partial shade; full sun makes the water too hot and allows algae to flourish.

In milder climates, fish can live in winter under a foot (30 cm) of ice with an air hole created by a pond heater, which is often called a "floating deicer." But if you live in an area with severe weather, take the fish inside in winter. Add snails, frogs, toads, and turtles to help control insects and algae.

INSTALL A WATERFALL For a waterfall, install a pump that circulates half the pond capacity per hour.

135

KNOW YOUR POND FISH

Common goldfish, comets, fantails, and oranda are all goldfish. They include dozens of varieties that can live up to 25 years. Common goldfish and comets have long, slender bodies and can grow to more than 12 inches (30 cm). They are fast-moving, hardy, and compatible with koi.

The common goldfish is the hardiest variety and can tolerate winter water temperatures as low as 35°F (2°C). They most often are bright orange, though some are yellow, silver, brown, or a mix.

Comets (A) are nearly as hardy as the common goldfish. Comets are longer and thinner than common goldfish, and their tails are longer. They can be gold, orange, brown, blue, red and white, orange and white, and orange and black. There also is a calico variety.

Fantails (B) and orandas (C) are considered fancy goldfish and have rounded, egg-shape bodies, and big fanlike tails. They grow about 5 inches (13 cm) long, but can get larger if given plenty of room. They do not mix well with larger, faster, more aggressive fish, such as common goldfish, comets, and Japanese koi. They tolerate water temperatures from 45° to 90°F (7°-32°C). Fantails come in many shapes and colors. Orandas are usually orange or red and may have some white. In adulthood, they develop a red or orange "crest" or "cap" on their heads.

Japanese koi (D), a member of the carp family, are available in red, orange, yellow, black, blue, and cream. Because of their bright colors, they are easy prey for predators, especially blue herons and raccoons. But with proper defenses, they are a joy of a pet, swimming to a pond's edge, where they are willing to be handfed–even petted–by people.

A

B

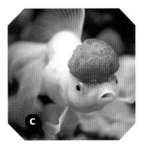
C

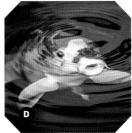
D

136

AVOID OVERCROWDING

There's no doubt about it: Fish add a magical quality to any water feature. Here's our guide to helping you choose the best fish:

Start by knowing how many fish your pond can handle. One general rule is to have 1 inch (2.5 cm) of fish for every 10 gallons (38 L) of water. So if your pond has about 50 gallons (190 L) of water, you can have one 6-inch-long (15 cm) fish, two 3-inch-long (8 cm) fish, or six 1-inch-long (2.5 cm) fish. If you're not sure how much water your pond holds, it's better to underestimate rather than to have too many.

When purchasing fish, pay attention to the shop's environment. The cleaner the store and the ponds, the more likely it is the shop staff give the fish good care.

Avoid purchasing fish from a tank that has dead fish floating in it. That may be a sign that the fish are unhealthy or diseased. Also pay attention if any of the fish are sick. One common sign of a sick fish is if it hangs out alone and has clamped fins. Unhealthy fish may also be missing scales, bear sores, or have missing fins.

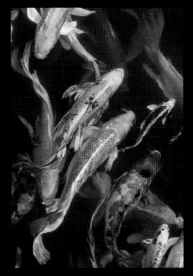

137

FENCE THE FLOWERS

A sturdy section of bentwood garden edging comes to the rescue of tall summer flowers. It's easy to make these flower supports with twigs and stems pruned from shrubs and small trees around the garden. These panels are taller than regular garden edging: Consider them portable miniature fence sections you can use just where you need them and for as long as they're needed. They are as handy in a vegetable and herb garden as they are among the daisies, and they're perfect for defining a border. After you make one, you'll find multiple ways to put it to work.

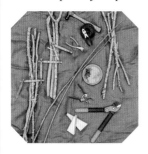

MATERIALS

Loppers; pruning shears; 3, 30-inch (76 cm) branches, approximately 1 inch (2.5 cm) in diameter; 3, 36-inch (91 cm) branches, less than 1 inch (2.5 cm) in diameter; 2, 25-inch (63.5 cm) branches, about ½ inch (1 cm) in diameter; 45-inch (114 cm) flexible whip or woody shoot; sallboard nails: 1½ inches (4 cm); hammer; 16-gauge tie wire; wire cutters; pliers; wire nails: 17 gauge, 1 inch (2.5 cm)

STEP 1 Lay out design using the 30-inch-long (76 cm) pieces as the upright posts. Set outside posts 30 inches (76 cm) apart; place the center upright slightly higher than the end posts. Lay the three 36-inch (91 cm) crosspieces on top, placing lowest crosspiece 12 inches (30 cm) above the bottom of the upright posts. Crosspieces will extend about 3 inches (8 cm) beyond posts on either side. The bottom of the center upright should be slightly below the lowest crosspiece.

STEP 2 Nail the crosspieces to each of the upright posts. If necessary, use scrap lumber wedges to support the stems and prevent stems from splitting while driving the nails. Turn the panel over. Snip pieces of wire long enough to wrap around the joints; use pliers to twist the wire, making tight joints. Do this at every junction between crosspieces and the posts.

STEP 3 Turn the panel face-up and position the ray pieces in a V-shape. Use wire nails to secure the rays to the crosspieces where they meet. Bend the long whip and place it on top of everything, nailing it onto the panel in at least three places. When you place your flower fence in the garden, dig small holes for the posts with a trowel. Firm the soil around the posts.

138

DRESS UP A WINDOW BOX

This simple design turns a narrow shutter attached to a cedar window box and a little yellow paint into a sunny container. Weather-hardy plants here include lantana (*Lantana camara* 'Tropical Fruit'), sedge (*Carex flagellifera* 'Toffee Twist'), and *coleus* (Coleus 'Rustic Orange').

139

MAKE A GARDENING STATION

Repurpose an old china cabinet (A) into a peppy potting bench with paint, tile, and clever DIY ideas.

First, remove doors, hardware, glass, and cabinet back (if possible). Separate top of cabinet from base. Fill any holes with wood putty and sand all surfaces.

Apply exterior primer to entire cabinet inside and out. When dry, paint the entire cabinet, then any doors and drawers that you have removed. If necessary for even coverage, apply a second coat.

Once paint is dry, measure any window panels you will be covering with chicken wire. Cut wire to fit, plus ¼ inch (6 mm) extra on each side. Attach wire to the back of the window with staples, then cover with wood trim and secure with pin nails. Screw on new knobs and drawer pulls. Reattach doors using new hinges.

Cut plywood to fit the cabinet top (what will become the work surface). Screw plywood to cabinet base. Adhere border to plywood using wood glue. Use a notched trowel to apply thinset adhesive to the top of the plywood.

ADHERE THE TILE (B, C) Place tile on the adhesive and let dry for 24 hours.

GROUT Mix grout according to package instructions. Use a rubber float to spread the grout mix over the surface to grout tile joints (D).

Once the grout is firm, use a damp sponge to wipe off excess (E). Allow the grout to set for 24 hours. Apply grout sealer according to package directions.

SECURE Attach the hutch to the cabinet base; reattach the back. Add hooks to hold hose and other garden tools if desired. Place the finished workstation on a covered patio or other outdoor space where it will be protected from the elements.

PROTECTIVE PAINT The exterior primer and paint will help protect the hardworking potting bench.

HOOK UP Hooks screwed to supports inside the cabinet and on the door keep frequently used garden implements handy; the shelves hold pots, gloves, and other supplies (F).

WIRE WINDOWS Ditch the old cabinet hardware in favor of fun decorative knobs to update and personalize the piece (G) and replace door panels with see-through chicken coop wire.

TILED TOP The exterior-grade plywood top covered in tile makes the cabinet workworthy.

HANDY HOSE Keep water close to your work space (H). We used two vintage coat hooks drilled into a support board inside the cabinet to create a handy hose holder.

140

SAVE WATER WITH A RAIN BARREL

Cheap, simple, and smart: Making a rain barrel is an easy project that takes just a few tools and supplies. That saved water can be used for containers and flowerbeds. Here's how to do it:

To make a rain barrel you'll need a drill; a large plastic barrel or container with lid; a spigot; 2 metal washers; 2 rubber washers; a tube of waterproof sealant or roll of plumbers tape; hose clamp; scissors; and landscaping fabric.

STEP 1 Drill a hole near the bottom of the barrel to insert the spigot. Use a drill bit that's the same size or slightly smaller than the spigot. The hole should be placed high enough that you have space to fill a watering can.

STEP 2 Place a metal washer onto the threaded end of the spigot, then place a rubber washer over the threads to help hold the metal washer in place and prevent leakage.

STEP 3 Apply a bead of waterproof sealant or plumbers tape over the rubber washer, then insert the spigot into the hole. Wait for the sealant to dry, then run a rubber washer, followed by a metal washer, onto the threads of the spigot inside the barrel. Secure the spigot in place inside the barrel using the hose clamp.

STEP 4 Cut a hole in the lid where the water will run directly into the barrel from a downspout. Be sure the hole is large enough to accommodate the water flow from the downspout.

STEP 5 Drill one or two holes near the top of the rain barrel to allow water to overflow.

STEP 6 With sturdy scissors, cut a piece of landscaping fabric to fit over the top of the barrel, then place the lid on top to secure the fabric. This creates a barrier to keep out mosquitoes and other pests.

STEP 7 Place the barrel directly underneath a downspout. You also can set it up on a platform to help add more pressure if you connect it to a hose. That also makes filling a watering can easier.

141

SET UP A GREENHOUSE

SITE Consider how you will access water and electricity. If you plan to hook up to household utilities, make it as convenient and cost-effective as possible.

WATER A misting or drip watering system proves efficient, but most gardeners use a hose or watering can.

LIGHT Plants needing the most light can be placed on tables or suspended from the roof. Lower-light plants and those that prefer cooler conditions can be placed on the floor and under tables. Supplemental light and heat may be necessary.

HEAT The plants grown in your greenhouse will depend on its minimum winter temperature. A warm (60°F to 70°F [16°C–21°C]) environment requires heating to maintain temperatures during bitterly cold nights, but it's ideal for orchids and hibiscus. A cool (minimum 50°F [10°C]) greenhouse suits many plants, including jasmine and citrus.

AIR Humidity is usually higher in a greenhouse, so it may not be the best place for succulents. A fan bolsters essential air movement. Budget for automated ventilation or open a door, window, or manual vent to let in fresh air on warm days.

SUPERVISION Keep the space clean and quarantine new plants. Watch for signs of pests and diseases, so you can fix the situation promptly.

142

CREATE A PERFECT COTTAGE GARDEN

STEP 1 Site a traditional cottage garden near the house in a mostly sunny area with rich, well-drained soil.

STEP 2 Make a flexible plan to create underlying order in the seeming chaos of flowers and plants.

STEP 3 Enclose at least part of the garden with fencing or walls.

STEP 4 Work with traditional materials such as wood, stone, and local brick for hardscaping.

STEP 5 Combine fruit trees, herbs, and other practical edibles with ornamentals for a historical cottage garden. The pictured modern interpretation uses a mix of evergreen and deciduous trees and shrubs, flowers, edibles, and architectural pieces.

STEP 6 Add sheared boxwood to give your cottage garden structure and winter color.

STEP 7 Cultivate self-sowing annuals, biennials, and perennials such as foxglove, lady's mantle, cosmos, marigolds, and Brazilian verbena (Verbena bonariensis) for spontaneous plant combinations.

STEP 8 Plant perennials in irregular sweeps and groups to simulate nature.

STEP 9 Use see-through fillers, such as gaura and baby's breath, in empty spaces for a full, lush look.

STEP 10 Complete the classic cottage garden look with roses.

143 GO NATIVE

Create a colorful flower garden with hardy native plants that will thrive even in less than ideal conditions.

FALSE INDIGO Bushy plants with bold purple-blue spikes brighten the late-spring border. Average soil; 5 feet (1.5 m) tall and 2 feet (60 cm) wide.

IRONWEED Vibrant purple blooms bring beneficial insects to the late-summer garden. Full sun; average soil; 6 feet tall (1.8 m) and 2 feet (60 cm) wide.

MAIDENHAIR FERN Lovely in woodland gardens. Partial to full shade; average to moist soil; 16 inches (40 cm) tall and 16 inches (40 cm) wide.

BUTTERFLY WEED A food source for the larvae of monarch butterflies. Full sun; average to dry soil; 36 inches (90 cm) tall; 2 feet (60 cm) wide.

QUEEN OF THE PRAIRIE Cotton-candy bloom clusters in summer top tall, sturdy stems. Full sun; average to wet soil; 8 feet (2.4 m) tall and 4 feet (1.2 m) wide.

JOE PYE WEED This show-stopping prairie native grows 4 to 6 feet (1.2–1.8 m) tall and prefers moist soil. It flowers in late summer.

CANADIAN WILD GINGER A velvet-leaf groundcover thrives in woods. Partial to full shade; average to moist soil; 6 inches (15 cm) tall and 6 inches (15 cm) wide.

CULVER'S ROOT Elegant white spires in midsummer attract bees. Full sun to light shade; average to moist soil; 6 feet (1.8 m) tall and 18 inches (46 cm) wide.

GOLDENROD Beneficial insects love these fall-flowering beauties. Full sun; average, well-drained soil; 2 inches (5 cm) to 6 feet (1.8 m) tall and 8 to 36 inches (20-90 cm) wide .

BEE BALM Bright summer blooms draw plenty of attention, and hummingbirds too! Full sun to light shade; average to moist soil; 4 feet (1 m) tall and 18 inches (46 cm) wide. .

GAILLARDIA Also called blanket flower, gaillardia is a heat- and drought-tolerant perennial wildflower that grows 2 feet (60 cm) tall. Blooms summer into fall.

PURPLE CONEFLOWER This prairie native offers large sturdy daisylike flowers with dropping petals. Draws birds, bees, and butterflies. Grows 1 to 8 feet (30.5–244 cm) tall.

144

HANDCRAFT A HANDBARROW

The handbarrow is no newcomer to the homestead. Documented at least as far back as the Middle Ages, this traditional tool makes it simple for two people to move unwieldy plants. Old versions of the barrow sometimes consisted of side-by-side slats with no enclosed tray. We made ours with sides to help keep plants from slipping off and with legs to make it easier to set down.

You'll need enough 1×4 (2.5× 10 cm) lumber (about 19 feet [5.8 m] overall) to make the sides, ends, and bottom in lengths; four 14-inch-long (36 cm) 2×2s (5×5 cm) for legs; saw; drill; hammer and nails; screwdriver; eight 2-inch-long (5 cm) coated wood screws; sandpaper; linseed oil stain; latex paint; paintbrush; and a band saw (optional)

GET A GRIP The barrow essentially is a long-handle tray with legs. To begin, cut two 48-inch-long (1.2-m) 1×4s (2.5× 10 cm) for the sides. Create handles by cutting out curves with a saw or band saw. Sand the edges so they're rounded and feel good in your hands.

PROVIDE THE SIDES Cut two 18-inch-long (46 cm) 1×4s

(2.5× 10 cm) for the ends. Attach them to the sides with wood screws, positioning them 12 inches (30 cm) from the handle ends and 23 inches (59 cm) apart. Drill pilot holes to prevent splitting.

GIVE IT LEGS Taper the bottom 10 inches (25 cm) of the four legs slightly using a band saw. Position the legs in each of the corners flush with the top of the tray as shown. Nail in place from sides and ends, drilling pilot holes if needed.

ADD THE BOTTOM To make the bottom, cut four 1×4s (2.5× 10 cm) to a length of 23 inches

(59 cm) each. (Note: Boards should fit tightly between tray ends; adjust board length if needed.) Notch two of the boards to fit around the legs, as shown. Drive the boards in place in the tray bottom; nail in place from each end. Keep gaps between the boards to aid drainage.

PAINT YOUR BARROW Sand slightly. Treat the entire barrow with stain; let dry. Mix a small amount of sawdust into your paint (this will help create a rough, weathered appearance); apply the paint to the barrow. When dry, sand off some paint for a vintage look.

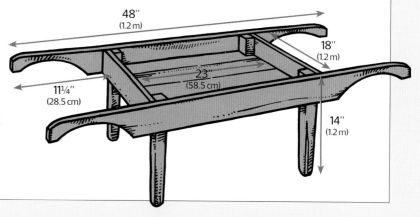

145

HEAT WITH FIREWOOD

Heating with wood provides an off-the-grid solution to staying warm during even the worst winters. A wood fire can provide zone heating, backup heat, and a main source of heat. Wood, sustainably harvested and properly dried, is a green way to heat. Wood also can be an athletic choice for heating when you count the splitting, stacking, and carrying. If you cut your own trees, add a fourth workout.

With these pointers, you should be on your way to warming your toes by the fire.

WHAT TO BURN

Some 60 percent of wood is water when the tree first comes down, but different tree species have different moisture contents. Wood from deciduous trees, or hardwoods, is what you want. Some of the best species are black locust, hickory, and oak. Maple, beech, and birch are sold more frequently as firewood, but species availability varies by region. Avoid burning softwood, or wood from coniferous trees like fir, pine, and cedar, which have high-moisture contents and give off more chimney-fouling creosote. No matter what wood you choose, make sure it's dry before you burn it.

BUYING WOOD

Wood sells green (wet) or dry. You can buy it cut to fit your woodstove or, if you're feeling ambitious,

tree-length to cut for yourself. Cut-to-fit wood comes split or round. Firewood is sold by the cord or fraction of a cord. A cord is a stack that is 4 feet×4 feet×8 feet (1.2 m×1.2 m×2.4 m). Because wood is irregular, it's impossible to stack it perfectly, and that's why a cord is an approximate measurement.

Wood can often be delivered by the dealer. Make sure to obtain a signed receipt of what's being delivered in case you discover a problem in volume or dryness later.

Look for dry wood to be gray with bark that peels at the ends. When you bang two pieces of dry wood together, you should hear a hollow sound.

STORING WOOD

Split unsplit wood as soon as possible. An automatic splitter is an option if you don't want to use an ax. Rent a splitter for a couple of days and save yourself backbreaking labor.

Buy firewood nine months to a year in advance. In warm months, stack the wood in a dry and sunny spot. Keep the wood off the ground by putting it on top of pallets or poles. Leave enough space between stacks for air to flow. Cover the top of the wood with a plastic tarp, but don't cover the sides. Before the snow falls, collect a good supply of kindling. Make sure your chimney is clean before the fire season too.

Index

weldon**owen**

PRESIDENT & PUBLISHER Roger Shaw
SVP, SALES & MARKETING Amy Kaneko

ASSOCIATE PUBLISHER Mariah Bear
ASSOCIATE EDITOR Ian Cannon

CREATIVE DIRECTOR Kelly Booth
ART DIRECTOR Allister Fein
SENIOR PRODUCTION DESIGNER Rachel Lopez Metzger

ASSOCIATE PRODUCTION DIRECTOR Michelle Duggan
IMAGING MANAGER Don Hill

Waterbury Publications, Inc., Des Moines, IA
CREATIVE DIRECTOR Ken Carlson
EDITORIAL DIRECTOR Lisa Kingsley
ART DIRECTOR Doug Samuelson
SENIOR EDITOR Tricia Bergman
PRODUCTION ASSISTANT Mindy Samuelson

MEREDITH CORE MEDIA
Editorial Content Director Doug Kouma
Brand Leader Karman Hotchkiss
Creative Director Michelle Bilyeu
BUSINESS ADMINISTRATION
Vice President/Group Publisher Scott Mortimer
Executive Account Director Doug Stark

© 2017 Weldon Owen inc.
1045 Sansome Street, San Francisco, CA 94111
www.weldonowen.com

Weldon Owen is a division of Bonnier Publishing USA

Library of Congress control number on file with the publisher.

ISBN 978-168188-233-8
10 9 8 7 6 5 4 3 2 1
2017 2018 2019 2020 2021
Printed in China